My Church: P

Work for Her Unity.

Ada Chukwukeme

My Church: Pray for Her Unity, and Work for Her Unity.

My Church: Pray for Her Unity, and Work for Her Unity.
Ada Chukwukeme

Summary: The need and the urgency for the Body of Christ to unite as Christ mandated and some clarification on misunderstanding about the Catholic Church.

10 digits ISBN 1497510880
13 digits ISBN 9781497510883

For most update: Read the postscript at the back of the book.

Visit the book's website: www.TheBoc13.com, and like us.

Appreciation

This book would never have been possible without the Blessed Trinity: God the Father, God the Son, and God the Holy Spirit! I thank the Blessed Trinity for the part each played in my salvation and that of mankind. Also, for these wonderful people my late parents Mazi & Mrs. E.N. Onwukeme, my siblings; and the diligence of several people who reviewed, edited, and made the publication of this book possible: Fr. Mary Patrick, O.C.S.O, Fr. Charles Cummings, O.C.S.O., Msgr. J. Terrence Fitzgerald, Vicar General, Emeritus; Msgr. Robert Servatius, Philip & Laurie Hofstetter, Barbara S. Lee, Deirdre Teodosio, Sharon Jackson, Michelle Valdez and Lisa Horowitz.

Dedication

This book is dedicated to my late parents Mazi Edmund N. & Mrs. Grace U. Onwukeme, my family, and the Bride of Christ universal.

Introduction:

There are many ways Catholic Christians and non-Catholic Christians are the same in our faith in our Lord and Savior Jesus Christ and there are some differences. These differences I need to explain to our non-Catholic brethren. The aim is for our non-Catholic brethren to read, pray and ask our Lord Jesus Christ if what they read in this book is true. By God's special grace the Holy Spirit will bear witness of His work. Consequently, we need to reconcile and embrace each other as brethren as quickly as possible to win more souls for Christ without wasting time. Time is of essence since we do not know the date or the hour of His second coming. As we do this our Heavenly Father, the Alpha and the Omega, the Almighty will pour out His Holy Spirit upon us to accomplish His plans and purposes at this point in human history.

My name is Elizabeth Ada Chukwukeme, I was born Elizabeth Ada Onwukeme in Jos, Nigeria. I attended Queen's School, Enugu, Nigeria. I studied Early Childhood Education at Howard University; received a Masters degree in Interactive Technology at Harvard University; and did a post graduate course in publishing procedures at Radcliffe College. All post secondary education were in the United States of America.

For over twenty (20) years I have worked in America and in Nigeria in various areas and capacities in education - teacher's aide, teacher, guest speaker, principal, school board, and founder/proprietress of a pre-school and an elementary school. Also, I have worked as a docent and a guest speaker at museums, and public libraries.

I love God and I enjoy travelling. As I travel I take the opportunity and hand out gospel tracts on streets, on buses, taxis, trains, canoes, and in airplanes; from Nigerian motor parks, airports in Europe to an Olympic football stadium in America. I will mention three experiences I had regarding God's goodness as I evangelized through gospel tracts.

The first experience is God's divine protection. When we do dangerous (things unknown to us) for the love of God He protects us. On several occasions I participated in evangelism outreaches with fellow Christians in Badagry Riverine area of Lagos, Nigeria, on a canoe powered by a small electric generator; there were no life jackets in the canoe, and I cannot swim. The water is home to crocodiles. I never thought of the idea that the canoe might capsize due to a rainstorm or the wind. When I was told by one of my brothers not to go, I did not give up going. Reflecting on those days, I saw the hand of God protecting me; there was no mishap.

The second experience was God's compassion. A few minutes before a train approaches the station I normally get up to distribute tracts. On a train from Chicago to New York I got up to distribute some tracts on this trip; however, it was laid in my heart to wait till 1.00 p.m. "I thought well by 1.00 p.m. the people will be gone and I will miss them." I sat down. At exactly 1.00 p.m., the train came to a complete halt a few yards away from the station. I stood up and began to distribute the tracts. Immediately after I finished the train began to move. I rejoiced in my heart and thanked God for His compassion for me to distribute the tracts with ease and for safety. On my trip from New York to Chicago I had distributed the tracts while the train was in motion. It was uneasy walking in-between cars.

The third experience is regarding God's sense of humor. In-flight to the States I was distributing tracts and a man asked me who gave me permission to distribute tracts. Not to be distracted I motioned to him on my way back that I will tell him. As I passed him, it was laid in my heart if he asks me who gave me permission I should ask him who gave him permission to speak to me. On the way back to my seat he never asked me because my answer will silence him. I guess he figured that out himself.

Our awesome God in His infinite mercy has done many wonderful things for me. He has rescued me as a child from a kidnapper and survived a civil war. As a young adult I was saved from drowning and divinely prevented from a plane crash; survived bullets wounds from hired assassins. As an adult living alone I was divinely awakened from sleep as the mattress I was sleeping on caught fire from a candle; and escaped armed robbers twice on the road. I was divinely healed of adenoma: a tumor on the thyroid gland; a goiter (caused by a lack of iodine) by drinking anointing oil; a kidney affected by gunshot was healed wholly during a Holy Ghost Service, at the Redeemed Christian Church of God in Jos, Nigeria.

Blessed be the Name of our Lord God Almighty; the Sovereign of the Universe; King Eternal; Immortal, Invisible, the Only Wise God; Who is, Who was, Who is to Come, the Almighty, for His tender mercies towards me.

Due to the last act of violence, I was led to leave Nigeria and come to the United States. I had planned to go to schools to read my book *Why Turtles Have Patchy Shells* and get into educational research or a teaching job to update my visa status and to send money to run the school I had founded.

But God had a different plan for me as I reflect on things. I was turned down numerous times for teaching jobs. I tried opening a Day Care and After School Program, but it did not work out.

Thus, without a major source of income in a foreign land our Great God had seen me through for eight years. I have worked with children and adults with my book; discovered the treasure trove in the Catholic Church. To keep my mind active and sane, I have developed numerous educational activities for various age groups and wrote several manuscripts for children's stories. I thank God for His mercy and goodness. It is not by my power nor my might but by the Spirit of the Almighty God! Our God is perpetually good and merciful.

How I came back to the Catholic Church and began praying the Rosary:

I was born and baptized in the Catholic Church; later in my early teens I was born again and was baptized by immersion in an Evangelical Church. I have fellowshipped and became part of different Christian denominations. I have served as a Sunday school teacher, a chorister; leaders in evangelism department and prayer department; an assistant pastor and ordained a deaconess.

In December of 2004, I was fasting and praying for 2005, asking the Lord for the Scripture He has for me for the New Year (2005). He gave me Revelations 12. Every day in the year 2005 I will read it to see what I could glean from this particular Scripture passage. Later it turned out to be one of the key passages that lead me back to the Catholic Church in 2005, and praying the Rosary.
The books I read in March and April of 2005 had a great impact on me: *The Rule of St. Benedict; Practicing His Presence; Miracles of the Eucharist;* and later *The Incorruptibles.*

In *The Rule of St. Benedict* I read how the monks are to fast on their words, and I remembered in one of the classes I took at the School of Disciples run by the Redeemed Christian Church of God, I learned about fasting on my words.

In *Practicing His Presence* I was captivated by Brother Lawrence (b.1614 – d. 1691) who was a lay brother in a Carmelite monastery in Paris; the book was based on his life testimony of the beauty in the Adoration of the Blessed Sacrament.

In *Miracles of the Eucharist* the sacredness and power in the Eucharist are indisputable. As a result of what I learned, I cancelled a meeting so I could attend the 10th Eucharistic Congress in Atlanta, Georgia.

In *The Incorruptibles* I learned about the Catholic saints who were found incorrupt many years after their death. It reminded me of what a group of women and I use to say to each other at a Christian fellowship "That our body will not see corruption just like in Psalm 16:10 "*For You will not leave my soul in shoel, nor will you allow your holy one to see corruption.*" New King James Version

With these discoveries I was absolutely very excited about the Catholic Church, my quest to attend the 10th Eucharistic Congress in Atlanta, Georgia; despite the fact that I had a round trip ticket to go to a networking gathering of Harvard alumni in New York City in the publishing industry. Good place for schmoozing to get something going as I had just arrived in the States from Nigeria in February of 2005. Instead I decided to attend the Eucharistic Congress to get a first hand touch on the Blessed Sacrament I have read so much about, although I had a sore throat and a hoarse voice; I refused home remedy or over the counter medication for a cure. Due to the stories I heard about the Catholic Church that were not good, I said to myself, "I will attend the healing seminar to know more about the power in the Eucharist." It is not that I have not tasted the power of Holy Communion in the Pentecostal denomination.

At the Eucharistic Congress on the Healing Seminar, Sr. Briege McKenna O.S.C gave a talk about how the power of the priest and power in the Eucharist were attacked in the 12th / 13th Century. She gave a testimony on how a child she had picked up from the dump on her way to Mass was healed during the Consecration of bread and wine, and the subsequent healing of people with cancer during the Adoration of the Blessed Sacrament in her seminars.

At the Eucharistic Congress I went for Adoration of the Blessed Sacrament; and at Mass during Holy Communion I asked the Lord should I partake? I received a go ahead. When I learned I had to go through certain procedures to be able to receive Holy Communion; I did go through the procedures some months later. As I left that Saturday evening, June 4th 2005 my throat was clear and my voice was clear.

After the above experiences I decided to go back to the Catholic Church. I thought if all these were the truth why not join now, why wait, no need to delay; the Catholic Church is truly the Church Jesus Christ instituted before His Ascension. So the next day I went back to the Catholic Church.

In the course of things I was not comfortable with the Virgin Mary being called the Queen of Heaven as the Rosary is prayed. So I started asking questions. I was directed to read Revelation 12:1 – *"A great sign appeared in the sky, a woman clothed with the sun, with the moon under her feet, and on her head a crown of twelve stars."* I was told it was the Coronation of the Blessed Virgin Mary as the Queen of Heaven. Within me I was like "WOW" this is the first verse of the Scripture God gave me for 2005! I asked about the brothers of Jesus, I was referred to Ezekiel 44:1-2 *"Then he brought me back to the outer gate of the Sanctuary, facing the east, but it was closed. He said to me: This gate is to remain closed; it is not to be opened for anyone to enter by it; since the LORD, the God of Israel has entered by it, it shall remain closed."* I kept quiet.

Three or four days later as I read Revelation 12, the Scripture given to me for 2005, verse 17 seemed to jump out *"Then the dragon became angry with the woman and went off to wage war against the rest of her offspring, those who keep God's commandments and bear witness to Jesus."* It became clear that we the believers in Christ are those who keep God's commandments are the Blessed Virgin Mary's children! I was overwhelmed!

There is one thing I had asked God to do for me after reading one of Bishop David Oyedepo's (is the General Overseer of Living Faith International a worldwide Pentecostal denomination with headquarters in Lagos, Nigeria) books in the late 90s. My request to God was: "Lord, if there is anything I will do that will prevent me from seeing You let me die the day before so I do not get to do that thing." Thus, I will not get to do whatever will make me not to see God or live in error. If going back to the Catholic Church was evil or an error I would not be alive today since in 2005 I returned to the Catholic Church. He is a covenant keeping God.

Title: My Church: Pray for her Unity and work for her Unity.
Outline: Introduction

1. **How I received the title:**

The title of this book was not of my making or imagination; I was awakened from sleep at 3:26 a.m. on Tuesday, January 4th, 2011 in Atlanta, Georgia with the words, *"My Church: Pray for her Unity and Work for her Unity."* in my ears. I picked up my Bible the nearest thing at the bedside, and wrote it down and then went back to sleep. I did not think much about it. After I came back to the Catholic Church I have prayed and desired for the unity of the Body of Christ.

2. **Confirmation of the title:**

On Sunday, January 9th, 2011 I was helping Laurie Hofstetter a friend in her Religious Education class, in my parish located in a suburb of Salt Lake City, Utah. She gave out prayer cards to her students and I asked her for one. She shuffled the pack of prayer cards and then selected one and then changed her mind. She went to the box where the whole pack of prayer cards were and selected a card and gave it to me. The card reads thus:

(a.) "Saint Charles Borromeo c. 1538-1584 Feast day November 4th People of Faith"

(b.) "Charles was born into an aristocratic family in Italy. His uncle became Pope Pius IV. Charles, who became a priest, bishop, and cardinal, worked hard to correct the mistakes that had contributed to divisions within Christianity that resulted from the Protestant Reformation. Charles worked on the drafting of the catechism (Catechism of Catholic Church) produced by the Council of Trent. Because of his efforts to reform the training of priests, Saint Charles Borromeo is the patron saint of seminarians."

*(c.)*Prayer: *"Saint Charles, pray for us that we may work toward the unity of all Christians. Help us accept those whose beliefs differ from our own. Amen."*

After reading the card, I knew it was the hand of God behind my friend selecting the card. Our merciful God was really trying to get the message of January 4th 2011, across to me.

On Wednesday, January 12th, 2011 at a Bible Study a bowl filled with names of saints was passed around I picked Blessed Pier Giorgio Ferassati. On the piece of paper it was written: "Blessed Pier Giorgio Ferassati Italy, feast day July 4th:"*To live without faith, without a patrimony to defend, without a steady struggle for truth that is not living, but existing. Pray for young apostles and apostles.*"

With this it was confirmed again that I should to start writing on my faith journey back to the Catholic Church, from Pentecostal denominations I had been part of and share it with the Body of Christ that God wants us to unite.

Another confirmation came on Thursday, August 4th 2011. I was bored with what I was reading; so I decided to check an old copy of the *Intermountain Catholic Newspaper*, for Salt Lake City Diocese, Utah June 10, 2011 for any article I had not yet read: I came across an article by Rev. Langes Jamie Silva, STL, JCD titled

"First Personal Ordinariate for former Anglicans created in Rome: Part one in a series" on the 11th paragraph it reads thus – "*The term Anglican patrimony is difficult to define but it would include many of the spiritual writings, prayers, hymnody, and pastoral practices distinctive to the Anglican tradition that have sustained the faith and longing of many Anglican faithful for that very unity for which Christ prayed.*"

I have written extensively on this book when I discovered the article, I knew without a shadow of a doubt this was an encouragement from God to continue writing.

The song that played on my CD player as I wrote this section of the book was ***UNITED*** *Tear Down the Walls*, produced by Hill Song Music Australia with Integrity Music and Columbia Records.

3. **Need for unity:**

We need to come together as one, for the fulfillment of John 17:20-23 *"I pray not only for them, but also for those who will believe in Me through their word, so that they may all be one, as You, Father, are in Me and I in You, that they also may be in us, that the world may believe that You sent Me. And I have given them the glory You gave Me, so that they may be one, as we are one, I in them and You in Me, that they may be brought to perfection as one, that the world may know that You sent Me, and that You loved them even as you loved Me."*

Also in Genesis 11:6 it speaks of the power of unity *"then the Lord said: If now, while they are one people, all speaking the same language, they have started to do this, nothing will later stop them from doing whatever they presume to do."*

Furthermore Psalm 133:1-3 upholds the power in unity *"Behold, how good and how pleasant it is for brethren to dwell together in unity! It is like the precious oil upon the head, running down upon the beard, the beard of Aaron, running down on the edge of his garments. It is like the dew of Hermon, descending upon the mountains of Zion; for there the Lord commanded the blessing- Life forevermore." New King James Version*

There is a necessity for Unity. God has planned it for His purposes to be accomplished this time in history, Jesus Christ prayed it and God wants us to obey Him from the heart. May the Holy Spirit enlighten our darkness, and help us to obey God. The above Scriptures speak volumes.

As we come together, we will experience Ephesians 3:10 *"So that the manifold wisdom of God might now be made known through the church to the principalities and authorities in the heavens."* The power of God will be revealed just as in the Acts of the Apostles. The Eucharist and the Word are two of our greatest weapons, and are powerful in the hands of Christians.

Through the years the enemy crept in subtly and stole the weapons and tools God has given us by dividing the Body, thus weakening her. Most non-Catholic Christians do not believe in the Real Presence of Christ in the Eucharist. And we Catholics do not have a systematic Bible study for the laity to study the Word of God as non-Catholic Christians do.

Yes, there was an error but it does not necessitate a break away. Though Romans 8:28 says, *"All things work together for good to them that love God who are called according to His purpose."* Jesus Christ wants us to be united so the world may know that God the Father sent Him to earth to redeem mankind. Read John 21:15-17 together with John 15 and 17, the Word of God is imputable and infallible.

For an illustration as regards to the Church Jesus Christ instituted, the Israelites were God's covenant people to usher in Christ; their sin did not change the covenant. Instead as they repented they were delivered from their captors or oppressors. God did not raise another nation to take their place to usher in Christ on earth for our salvation.

Another illustration, Peter was entrusted with leadership although he denied Jesus Christ but John was with Jesus Christ from the Garden of Gethsemane till He was crucified and buried. Peter's actions did not change Jesus Christ's mind regarding who will lead the Church.

Some people in the Catholic Church erred, yes, but that does not stop it from being the Church Christ instituted on earth before He ascended into heaven.

Thus, it stands to reason that the Catholic Church whose history is traced back to Peter is the Church Christ instituted and wants us all to come back Home to! See **section 33 Appendix A** *Day Five of "Chaplet of Divine Mercy."*

It is time to look inward, fast and pray and ascertain what the Lord wants from His Church. Pray for one another and care for one another. Forgive one another, as love dictates. *"If you keep My commandments, you will remain in My love, just as I have kept My Father's commandments and remain in His love. I have told you this so that My joy might be in you and your joy might be complete. This is My commandment: love one another as I have loved you."* John 15:9-12

Paul in 1Corinthians 3:5 wrote, *"What is Apollos, after all and what is Paul? Ministers through whom you become believers, just as the Lord assigned each one. I planted, Apollos watered, but God caused the growth (increase). Therefore neither the one who plants nor the one who waters is anything but only God, Who causes the growth (increase)."* Remember Apollos was the one whom Aquila and Priscilla heard preaching, they took him and expounded the way of God more perfectly (Acts 18:26). See, we need to love one another in spirit and in truth. If anyone in authority is in error, pray for the person and in time the person will repent.

Which Church is without a limp? God created Adam & Eve, the devil tried to thwart the relationship, Jesus Christ chose the twelve, the devil infiltrated through Judas Iscariot, so when the devil tries to thwart God's plan for unity (John 17) let's dare the devil and work things out by the leading of the Holy Spirit. Pray for what you know is wrong, and for deliverance for that part of the Body of Christ.

4. The Goal of the book

The goal of this book is for the Body of Christ to understand one another. Catholic Christians and non-Catholic Christians to come together in unity as Jesus Christ intended. What you have discerned and learned by the Holy Spirit come share it with the Church. He gave us each gifts for one another that we may be fully functional and not dysfunctional. Everything belongs to Him.

Martin Luther saw error and in the process to correct it removed eleven books (four were put back later by the Protestants) from the Bible that contradicted some of his Lutheran teachings. This now gave birth to 33,000 Christian denominations (Allen Hunt 2010). The books in the Bible he removed have been used for about one thousand five hundred years, not counting the period they were read before the coming of Christ. I believe Christ read these books because I was led to Sirach 11:19 which says, *"When he says: 'I have found rest, now I will feast on my possessions,' he does not know how long it will be till he dies and leaves them to others."* This is similar to the Rich Fool in Luke 12:10-21.Two other passages were Tobit 13:16b-18 you find a reference of it in Revelation 21:10-21, and 1 Maccabees 7:17 reads, *"The flesh of your saints they have strewn and their blood they have shed round about Jerusalem, and there was no one to bury them."* This reference is in Psalm 79:3 which says, *"They have spilled their blood like water all around Jerusalem, and no one is left to bury them."*

In **section 21** of this book you will see a brief description of the seven original books in the Bible Martin Luther removed. Proverbs 22:28 tells us not to remove the ancient landmarks. These Scriptures that were removed are ancient spiritual landmarks to show us our spiritual heritage. For instance Maccabees has the history for why Hanukkah [Feast of Dedication John 10:22-23] a Jewish celebration still observed up to today was instituted. If Luther rejected Maccabees, because it is not in the Jewish canonical Bible, how can the Jews celebrate a feast which is not in their Bible? Maccabees 1 and 2 a true account of what happened in Jewish history. In Maccabees it tells of how the Greeks were burning their Scriptures and how some of them went about to preserve it. Maccabees is one of them.

In 2 Peter 1:20 – 21 it says, *"Know this first of all, that there is no prophecy of the Scripture that is a matter of personal interpretation, for no prophecy ever came through human will; but rather human beings moved by the Holy Spirit spoke under the influence of God."*

There are similarities and differences in what we profess to believe among all Christians; some of the major differences I will explain. These are the Mass, the Eucharist, the Blessed Virgin Mary, the Rosary, the Divine Mercy Chaplet, statues & stained glass, Stations of the Cross, the seven (7) books that Martin Luther removed from the Bible, to ask the saints to pray for us, to pray for the dead, purgatory, relics, confession, priests not marrying, women not ordained as priests and poverty/sufferings.

After reading please ask God through His Holy Spirit to reveal to you what to do. Each one of us will stand and give account of ourselves before Him; no man will do it for you or for me. Romans 14:12 "*So [then] each of us shall give an account of himself [to God].*"

5. The Old Path before the Division: The Order of Worship Service

The Mass was the mode of worship by the early Christians. Below is the testimony of Justin the Martyr given to Emperor Antonius Pius:

Justin the Martyr: *"On the day we call the day of the Sun, all who dwell in the city or country gather in the same place…*

The memoirs of the apostles and the writings of the prophets are read…

When the reader has finished, he who presides…admonishes & challenges them to imitate these beautiful things.

Then we all rise together and offer prayers for ourselves…and for all others…

Sign of peace with a kiss

Then, someone brings bread and a cup of water and wine mixed together to him who presides over the brethren

He takes them and offers praise and glory to the Father of the universe, through the name of the Son and the Holy Spirit and for a considerable time gives thanks (in Greek: Eucharistic) that we have been judged worthy of these gifts

When he has concluded the prayers and thanksgivings, all present give voice to an acclamation by saying: 'Amen.'

When he who presides has given thanks and the people have responded, those whom we call deacons give to those present the "Eucharistic" bread, wine and water and take them to those who are absent.

Because this bread and wine have been made [into the] Eucharist...no one may take part in it unless he believes that what we teach is true, has received baptism for the forgiveness of sins and new birth, and lives in keeping with what Christ taught.

For we do not take these things as ordinary bread or ordinary drink. Just as our Savior Jesus Christ was made flesh by the word of God and took flesh and blood for our salvation, so, also we were taught that food, for which thanksgiving has been made through the word of prayer instituted by Him, and from which our blood and flesh nourished after the change, is the flesh of that Jesus Who was made flesh."

{Justin the Martyr gives the Emperor [Antonius Pius] an overview of the structure of Mass and not every detail. From Apology I. 66-67ca. 150 AD.} Used with permission from Fr. James Flanagan.

The above resembles the present day Catholic Mass. The Catholic Mass is made up of two parts: Liturgy of the Word (which has its origins in ancient Jewish Synagogue service, see Luke 4:16-22), and the Liturgy of the Eucharist. The Liturgy of the Eucharist is based in part on the Last Supper of Jesus Christ and the Apostles which is rooted in Jewish Passover and further it memorializes the whole Paschal Mystery of Jesus, especially His death on the cross, resurrection, ascension and sending of the Holy Spirit. [Used with permission of Fr. Dan Merz.]

Jesus Christ instituted the Last Supper and commanded us to keep it. Eucharistia was the Greek word for thanksgiving. As Greek was the lingua-franca of the time, Eucharistia was first used to describe the worship service. The word Missa was later used. Missa is the Latin word for dismissal; it was used in reference to dismiss to mission.

The present word Mass was first used in recorded form by St. Ambrose (d. 397) in a letter to his sister Marcellina. Here is an excerpt from the letter, *"The next day (it was Sunday) after the lessons and the tract, having dismissed the catechumens, I explained the creed [symbolumtradebam] to some of the competents [people about to be baptized] in the baptistery of the Basilica. There I was told suddenly that they had sent soldiers to the Portiana Basilica... But I remained at my place and began to say Mass]."* (Catholic Encyclopedia www.newadvent.org, Kevin Knight used with permission.)

Malachi 1:11 foretells the celebration of Mass, *"For from the rising of the sun, even to its setting My name is great among the nations, and everywhere they bring sacrifice to My name, and a pure offering; for great is My name among the nations, says the Lord of Hosts."* Mass is celebrated from sun rise to sunset worldwide; each hour somewhere around the world, Mass is celebrated.

To substantiate the use of the word Mass: There are things instituted in worship services in the temple that were not instituted by Moses (e.g. King David instituted the temple choir. You find this in 1 Chronicles 6:16 *"The following were entrusted by David with the choir services in the Lord's house from the time when the ark had obtained a permanent resting place.")* By the leading of the Holy Spirit, King David instituted the choir.

Another example is Trinity; it is the best word to articulate God the Father, God the Son, and God the Holy Spirit. The word Trinity is not found in the Bible.

Finally on Mass I will quote an entry in a *Through the Year with Fulton Sheen* for June 17 titled Mass in Dachau "A priest who was in the German prison camp Dachau describes the Mass after all the German guards were in bed. He said, "Our lives were in danger if we were ever discovered. A young priest had to memorize the names of all those who had received communion, but it was forbidden for us to gather in groups for prayer. After night call and bed check, we would set out guards, darken the windows, and the lucky one to be chosen to celebrate for this momentous occasion would carefully brush his pathetic prison garb, put the stole over his shoulders, and by the small light of his smuggled candle begin the commemoration of that other great Passion of which our own was the physical continuation. We could understand the Mass. All that could crowd into the room were there, tears of joy running down our cheeks. Christ the Lord, who knew what suffering was, was coming to suffer with us, to bring us strength and consolation. The small hosts were broken into many particles as possible so the greatest number could communicate. We had to keep a secret roster of those who received. We missed some of the liturgy perhaps, but I think that God looked down into that prison room and found a particularly refreshing response to his cry of love from the cross, 'I thirst.' There was nothing that could keep us from doing all in our power to be closer to God." ©

6. **The cause for the division**:

One of the main causes for division was due to the selling of indulgences. Teaching that salvation is by works alone has been corrected. We need both faith and works to prove a change of heart and mind. Works make our faith effective. In Matthew 5:16 Jesus Christ said, *"Just so, your light must shine before others, that they may see your good deeds and glorify your heavenly father. James said without works our faith is dead.* In Revelation 19:8b reads thus, *"The linen represents the righteous deeds of the holy ones."*

7. **The correction:**

The Council of Trent (1545 – 1563) ratified the errors that caused the division. God used St. Charles Borromeo and others to correct what had caused the division, he started seminaries to train priests. He participated in the drafting of the catechism of the Catholic Church published by the Council of Trent. James 5:20 says ,*"He should know that whoever brings back a sinner from the error of his way shall save his soul from death, and will cover a multitude of sins."*

Please, read the Desert Fathers, the Church Fathers, St. Augustine, St. Francis of Assisi, St. Benedict, St. Patrick etc. Also these books Ladder of Divine Ascent, Practicing His Presence, Catechism of the Catholic Church any of these will unearth spiritual treasures in the Catholic Church. These saints, all worshipped in the Catholic Church!

8. **The Eucharist/Holy Communion:**

The unforgettable experience I had at the 10th Eucharistic Congress in Atlanta was a turning point for me back to the Catholic Church. I have tried to participate in daily Mass and adoration of the Blessed Sacrament as much as I can to nourish my soul. Each experience refreshes my heart and soul, fortifies me to live in peace and joy against all the odds.

In John 6:51-54 Jesus said, *"I Am the Living Bread that came down from heaven; whoever eats this bread will live forever; and the bread that I will give is My Flesh for the life of the world." The Jews quarreled among themselves saying, "How can this man give us His flesh to eat? Jesus said to them, 'Amen, Amen, I say to you, unless you eat the flesh of the Son of Man and drink His blood, you do not have life within you. Whoever eats My Flesh and drinks My Blood has eternal life, and I will raise him on the last day.'"*

At the Last Supper as Matthew26: 26 -28 records, "*While they were eating, Jesus took bread, said the blessing, broke it, and giving it to His disciples said,* ***"Take and eat; this is My Body." Then He took a cup, gave thanks, and gave it to them, saying, "Drink from it, all of you, for this is My Blood of the covenant, which will be shed on behalf of many for the forgiveness of sins."***

With the above statement Jesus said what he meant, and meant what He said. He did not just say it was a symbol. To substantiate this see the testimony of Justin the Martyr in **section 4**, also the *Miracles of the Eucharist,* by Joan C. Cruz. What I read made me want to attend the Eucharistic Congress in Atlanta. Below are three examples that influenced me from Joan C. Cruz's book on the reality of the Presence of Jesus Christ in the Eucharist/Holy Communion.

9. **The Miracles of the Eucharist**

A. Middleburg-Louvain, Belgium 1374 p.123

There was once a noble and wealthy lady who lived in Middleburg, Belgium. She was very gracious and devout, not only that she taught her helpers in the line.

It happened that on the first Sunday of Lent in 1374 she told her helpers to go to confession and to receive the Holy Communion. Jean of Cologne felt that he had to go so that he would not be humiliated or disgraced so he went to receive the Eucharist without going to confession. As the Sacred Host touched Jean's tongue it became flesh, and he was not able to swallow.

> He was afraid and could not hide it, he bit into it and blood started to drip from his lips and stained the cloth draped over the communion railing. The priest saw this and took the Host. He placed the Host in a golden vessel.

Jean became blinded immediately. Once he repented of his sacrilegious and confessed his sin, he regained his sight. The Archbishop of Cologne, Fredric III had the Host kept at the Cathedral. Later the Host was taken to the Augustinian monastery.

When the Prior Bayrens wanted to extend the devotions to the monastery of Louvain in Belgium, another miracle occurred when the Host split into two without human intervention. It is so remarkable because the thought of dividing the Host into two is quite disrespectful so the monks' prayed for three days, then the miracle happened!

The papers documenting the history, travels and examination of this miracle are still in the archives of St. Jaques Church.

B. Seefeld, Austria 1384 p. 130

There was a knight named Oswald Milser who was the guardian of Schlossberg castle in the northern part of Seefeld, Austria. He was full of himself due to his post and power. He had tremendous influence. Here is a record from the *Golden Chronicle of Hohenschwangau,* about his disrespect of the Blessed Sacrament.

"Oswald Milser came down with his followers to the parish Church of Seefeld. He demanded- and a refusal could mean death-the large Host; the small one he regarded as too ordinary for him. He surrounded the frightened priest and the congregation with armed men. At the end of Mass, Milser, his drawn sword and his head covered, came to the left of the high altar, where he remained standing. The stunned priest handed him the Host, upon which the ground under the blasphemer suddenly gave way. He sank up to his knees. Deathly pale, he grasped the altar with both hands, the imprints of which can be seen to this day.

The knight filled with fear motioned for the priest to take the Host out of his mouth. Immediately the priest removed the Host and the ground became firm. He swiftly left the Church and went to the monastery to confess his sin of pride.

A silver monstrance was made for the exposition of the miraculous Host. It is still preserved. The area where this miracle occurred is still there- the hollow where Oswald's knee sank, the impression of his hands that sank onto the side of the stone altar – are all visible to visitors."

C. "Miracle of the Year 1266" Santarem, Portugal 13th Century p.38

A poor woman, who lived in Santarem village a 30 to 35 minutes drive from Fatima, was mistreated by her husband by his unfaithfulness. It made her so miserable that she went to a sorceress, who told her to bring a consecrated Host.

Not willing to, initially, but later during Mass instead of consuming her Holy Communion she wrapped it with her veil. Suddenly, blood started to come out from the Host through the veil, people saw it. They came to help her thinking she hurt herself. She ran to avoid them, but the drops of blood followed her home.

She hid the veil and the Host in a trunk. However, at night light came out from the trunk and lit-up the whole house. The husband and the wife knelt and adored till morning. The parish priest was notified.

A committee was set up to look into the miracle. The Host was put in wax paper and secured in the tabernacle at St. Steven. Much later, when the tabernacle was opened there was another miracle: the wax paper was broken in pieces and the Host enclosed in a crystal pyx. It was later housed in a gold and silver pear-shaped monstrance with a "Sunburst" of 33 rays.

After the investigation, it was known that the miracle was genuine, the Church of St. Steven was renamed "The Church of Holy Miracle." A medical doctor, Arthur Hoagland from New Jersey has observed the miraculous Host many times for some years; these were his conclusions: the blood that collected at the base of the crystal from the Host has the color of fresh blood and sometimes and at other times that of dried blood. This miracle has lasted for over 700 years. *Miracles of the Eucharist* © by Joan C. Cruz; Tan Books, Charlotte, NC 28241 used with permission.

Another example, Brother Lawrence (c.1614 -12th February 1691) a lay brother in a Carmelite monastery in Paris; worked at the kitchen in the monastery where he belonged. Due to his character and spiritual insight people came to him for spiritual guidance. This is his comment about the Blessed Sacrament (Eucharist/Consecrated Host) "The time of business does not with me differ from the time of prayers; and in the noise and clatter of my kitchen, while several persons are at the same time calling for different things, I possess God in as great tranquility as if I were upon my knees at the Blessed Sacrament. I keep myself in His Presence by simple attentiveness and a loving gaze upon God which I can call the actual Presence of God or to put it more clearly, a habitual, silent and secret conversation of the soul with God."

Also, Bishop Fulton Sheen's writings were compiled into a yearly devotional; for January 21st entry titled The Secret of My Power - "When I stand up to talk, people listen to me; they will follow what I have to say. Is it any power of mine? Of course not. St. Paul says: "What have you that you have not received, why do you glory as if you had not?" But the secret of my power is that I have in fifty-five years not missed spending an hour in the Presence of our Lord in the Blessed Sacrament. That's where the power comes from. That's where sermons are born. That's where every good thought is conceived." I don't mean to say that these hours have always been good. I've had to walk up and down the Church to stay awake. I once went to St. Roch's Church in Paris to pray on my way to Lourdes. There were only about five days in a year when I could sleep in the day time, and this was one. I sat down at two o'clock, and I slept perfectly until three. When I awoke I said to the good Lord, "Did I make a holy hour? And my angel said, "Yes, that's the way the apostles prayed the first one."*Through the Year with Fulton Sheen* © Ignatius Press, San Francisco, CA used with permission.

In addition, Martin Luther, in 1529 engaged the question of transubstantiation in the famous conference at Marburg with Zwingli and other Swiss theologians; he maintained his view that Christ is present in the bread and wine of the Eucharist." See the following reference (www.BiblicalCatholic.com David Armstrong used with permission.)

Present day observation regarding the **Blessed Sacrament**, I read from a non-denominational website: www.elijahlist.com posted on August 27, 2008 by James Goll's prophetic word subheading *When we care for His Presence* *"When My people will care for, cherish, nurture and love the 'Bread of My Presence' like a parent does its new born child then revival will come."* This I believe is Adoration of the Blessed Sacrament/Eucharistic Bread. (Contact information for James Goll: info@ecountersnetwork.com)

Personally, I testify that truly as the bread and wine is consecrated during Mass it turns into the **Real Body and Blood, Soul and Divinity of Our Lord and Savior Jesus Christ**. If you put a gun or knife to my throat to deny it; I will not deny it! I have been prompted that it is real several times.

10. The Incorruptibles:

One of the books that I read that led to my coming back to the Catholic Church is the *Incorruptibles* by Joan C. Cruz. In this book, the saints in the Catholic Church whose bodies were found to be incorrupt when they were exhumed as part of the procedures for canonization are documented with extensive and thorough investigation. These men, women, and children adored the Blessed Sacrament and prayed the Rosary. I will list just a few below. For more please read the book, to discover some of the mysteries of God in His servants who have served Him without reservation and whom He has kept incorrupt by the power of His Word as it says in Psalm 16:10*"For you will not abandon me to sheol, nor let your faithful servant to see corruption."*

St. Bernadette Soubirous 1844-1879
St. Catherine of Siena 1347-11380
St. Albert the Great 1193/1206?-1280
St. Francis of Xavier 1506-1552
St. Rita of Cascia 1381-1457
St. Staislaus Kostka 1550-1568
St. Teresa of Avila 1515-1582

A modern day Catholic Blessed Pier Giorgio Ferassati 1901-1925 in the process of canonization, died on July 4th 1925, his body was found incorrupt in 1981 in his family tomb in the cemetery of Pollone and it was taken to the Cathedral of Turin.

Another modern day saint to mention is St. Padre Pio who lived from 1896 to 1968. He was a priest in Italy and God gave him a number of gifts: bi-location (ability to travel through the air like Philip [who after he ministered to the Ethiopian eunuch] travelled through the air to Azotus Acts 8:26-40), stigmata (wounds/pains at the points in the body where Christ was nailed to the Cross), and reading souls (at confession if one forgets a sin or too ashamed to mention it he reminds them of it).

11. The Blessed Virgin Mary:

Catholics do not worship or teach us to worship the Blessed Virgin Mary, the Mother of Jesus. Those who do, do it ignorantly. Rather, Catholics give her the honor due her as the Mother of God, because Jesus Christ is part of the Godhead, God the Father, God the Son and God the Holy Spirit. It stands to reason that she is the Mother of God our Lord Jesus Christ in the flesh. Elizabeth in Luke 1:43 said, *"And whence is this to me, that the Mother of my Lord should come to me?"* Elizabeth is much older than Mary it was the Holy Spirit and her humility that led her to address Mary as the Mother of my Lord!

The seed of the man and an egg of a woman form a child; the attributes of the two DNAs are in the child. The blood and the genes in Blessed Virgin Mary are of Immaculate Conception. In Genesis 3:15b it says, *"And I will put enmity between you and the woman, and between your seed and her Seed;"* The Seed is Jesus Christ, placed and activated in the womb of the Blessed Virgin Mary by the power of the Holy Spirit. Her blood is in Jesus Christ. Jesus was nursed by her. So food nutrients, blood, water, flowed from her to Jesus. So there is no taint in her blood. There are no evil inclinations or dispositions in her; if there were, they would be in Jesus. She was full of grace; Archangel Gabriel, who stands before God, carried the message from God to her. "And coming to her, he said, 'Hail, favored one! The Lord is with you.' But she was greatly troubled at what was said and pondered what sort of greeting this might be'" Luke 1:28 - 29; see Luke 1:30 – 38 for the full message.

Another reason to honor her, God cannot risk handing over His Son to a woman who He cannot trust to teach His Son the precepts of His Word as a Child growing up in Israel and who will influence Jesus Christ negatively by our sin nature. Jesus depended on her for everything from conception, birth, toddler years, childhood years, pre-teen, teen years, till He left the house for His ministry. The Blessed Virgin Mary carried God the Son, she lived with Him, and He depended on her!

Reflecting on the wedding in Cana, Jesus said to the Blessed Virgin Mary, *"Woman, how does your concern affect Me? My hour has not come."* Jesus referred to her as "the woman" as mentioned in Genesis 3:15 as My time to reveal My identity as the Messiah. Besides Jesus did perform the miracle as she requested and His disciples began to believe in Him. It was not disrespect. When the hour came, Jesus did not shrink from it as recorded in Luke 22:14 *"When the hour came, He took His place at the table with the apostles."*

Next, at the Crucifixion John 19:26-27 *"When Jesus saw His Mother and the disciple there* whom he loved, He said to His Mother, *"Woman, behold, your son."* Then he said to the disciple, *"Behold, your mother." And from that hour the disciple took her into his home."* If the Blessed Virgin Mary had other children they would have taken her according to Jewish law. And someone who raised Jesus to have rebellious children who would not care for their mother is ridiculous. Here Jesus is sharing His Mother with us, just as He shared His Father with us. She stood with Him from birth to death. Simeon prophesied Luke 2:35 *"And you yourself a sword will pierce so that the thoughts of many will be revealed."* On Good Friday, from His trial to the tomb especially at the foot of the cross surely a sword certainly did pierce her; how could it not?

Furthermore, in Revelation 12:1 *"A great sign appeared in the sky, a woman clothed with the sun, with the moon under her feet, and on her head a crown of twelve stars."* The Blessed Virgin Mary having accomplished her task successfully with excellence on earth with no casualty or error was crowned as the Queen of Heaven and Earth. She was assumed into heaven body and soul. If Enoch and Elijah were taken up how much more the Mother of God! Let us not be biased because it was not written in the gospels. Well the people whom God revealed it to said so, in faith believe and do not be short changed by the devil; because her intercession is powerful.

Mary is the Queen of Heaven and Earth, but she is not the one mentioned in Jeremiah 7:18 *"The children gather wood, their fathers light the fires, and the women knead dough to make cakes for the queen of heaven, while libations are poured out to strange gods in order to hurt Me."* The queen of heaven mentioned in Jeremiah was the goddess of Assyro-Babylonian Ishtar, goddess of fertility, whose worship was introduced under King Manasseh and was revived after King Josiah's death. The Blessed Virgin Mary was not yet in the picture that is, not yet physically born. If there is no original there will be no counterfeit; if there is no $300.00 dollar bill, there will be no counterfeit of it. If one offers a $300.00 bill as a legal tender you know right away that it is a counterfeit because there is no original. The Blessed Virgin Mary is truly the Queen of Heaven and Earth, and her Son is the KING of kings.

Another reason to honor the Blessed Virgin Mary as our mother is found in Revelations 12:17 it says, *"Then the dragon became angry with the woman and went off to wage war against the rest of her offspring, those who keep God's commandments and bear witness to Jesus."* Here it points out that the rest of her offspring are the Christians who keep God's commandments. If Eve is the mother of the human race, Mary is the Mother of Christianity, Mother of the Church. She gave birth to our Savior. She has all the qualities of the new creation in Christ.

Jesus Christ said in John 16:12-15, *"I have much more to tell you, but you cannot bear it now. But when He comes, the Spirit of truth, He will guide you to all truth. He will not speak of His own, but He will speak what He hears, and will declare to you the things that are coming. He will glorify Me, because He will take from what is Mine and declare it to you."*

Finally, Martin Luther had nothing against the Blessed Virgin Mary or the Rosary. It was his followers who did not like both, so they removed them. See **section 12 below**.

12. **Martin Luther's and other Reformers' comments about the Blessed Virgin Mary:**

"On the feast of the Assumption August 15, 1552 Luther said: "There can be no doubt that the Virgin Mary is in heaven. How it happened we do not know. And since the Holy Spirit has told us nothing about it, we can make no article of faith…It is enough to know that she lives in Christ."

"The veneration of Mary is inscribed in the very depths of the human heart." (Sermon, September 1, 1522).

"No woman is like you. You are more than Eve or Sarah, blessed above all nobility, wisdom, and sanctity." (Sermon Feast of Visitation 1537)

"One should honor Mary as she herself wished and as she expressed it in the Magnificat. She praised God for His deeds. How then can we praise her? The true honor of Mary is the honor of God, the praise of God's grace… Mary is nothing for the sake of herself, but for the sake of Christ… Mary does not wish that we come to her, but through her to God." (Explanation of the Magnificat, 1521)

"It is consolation and super abundant goodness of God, that man is able to exult in such a treasure. Mary is His Mother…" (Sermon, Christmas, 1522).

"Mary is the Mother of Jesus and the Mother of all of us even though it was Christ alone Who reposed on her knees… If He is ours, we ought to be in His situation; there where He is, we ought also to be and all that He ought to be ours, and his Mother is also our Mother." (Sermon, Christmas, 1529).

On Mary's Immaculate Conception Luther writes – "It is a sweet and pious belief that the infusion of Mary's soul was effected without original sin; so that in the very infusion of her soul, she was also purified from original sin and adored with God's gifts, receiving a pure soul infused by God; thus from the moment she began to live she was free from all sin." (Sermon: On the day of the Conception of the Mother of God, 1527).

"She is full of grace, proclaimed to be entirely without sin-something exceedingly great. For God's grace fills her with everything good and makes her void of all evil. (Personal {"Little} Prayer Book, 1522)

On Perpetual Virginity Luther says, "Christ… was the only Son of Mary, and the Virgin Mary bore no children besides Him… I am inclined to agree with those who declare that 'brothers' really mean 'cousins' here, for the Holy Writ and the Jews always call cousins brothers." {Pelikan, ibid.v.22:214-15/Sermons on John, Chapters 1-4 (1539)}

"A new lie about me is being circulated. I am supposed to have preached and written that Mary, the Mother of God, was not a virgin either before or after the birth of Christ…" {Pelikan, ibd. V.45:199/That Jesus Christ was born a Jew (1523)}

"Scripture does not say or indicate that she later lost her virginity…"

"When Matthew [1:25] says that Joseph did not know Mary carnally until she had brought forth her Son, it does not follow that he knew her subsequently; on the contrary, it means that he never did know her… this babble… is without justification… he has neither noticed nor paid any attention to either Scripture or common idiom." {Pelikan, ibid. v.45:206, 212-3/That Jesus Christ was born a Jew (1523)}

"Christ our Savior was the real and natural fruit of Mary's Virginal womb… This is without the cooperation of man, and she remained a virgin after that." (REF: on the Gospel of John: Luther's Works, Vol.22.p.23, ed. Jaroslaw Pelikan, Concordia, 1957)

John Calvin's View: "Helvidius displayed excessive ignorance in concluding that Mary must have had many sons, because Christ's 'brothers' are sometimes mentioned." {Harmony of Matthew, Mark and Luke, sec.39 (Geneva, 1562), vol.2/From Calvin's Commentaries, tr. William Pringle, Grand Rapids, MI: Eerdmas, 1949, p.215; on Matt. 13:55}

On Matthew 1:25 **Calvin** writes, "The inference he [Helvidius] drew from it was, that Mary remained a virgin no longer that till her first birth, and that afterwards she had other children by her husband... No just and well – grounded inference can be drawn from these words... as to what took place after the birth of Christ. He is called 'first born;' but it is for the sole purpose of informing us that He was born of a virgin... What took place afterwards the historian does not inform us... No man will obstinately keep up the argument, except from extreme fondness of disputation." {Pringle; ibid. vol. 1, p.107}

"Under the word 'brethren' the Hebrews include all cousins and other relations, whatever may be the degree of affinity." {Pringle, ibid. vol.1, p.283/Commentary on John, (7:3)}

Huldreich Zwingli's View: "He turns, in September 1522, to a lyrical defense of the perpetual virginity of the Mother of Christ... To deny that Mary remained 'inviolata' before, during and after the birth of her Son was to doubt the Omnipotence of God... and it was right and profitable to repeat the angelic greeting – not prayer- 'Hail Mary...' God esteemed Mary above all creatures, including the saints and angels- it was her purity, innocence and invincible faith that mankind must follow. Prayer, however, must be... to God alone..."

'Fidei exposition,' the last pamphlet from his pen... There is a special insistence upon the perpetual virginity of Mary. {G.R. potter, Zwingli, London: Cambridge Univ. Press, 1976, pp.88-9, 395/The Perpetual Virginity of Mary..., September 17, 1522} Zwingli had printed in1524 a sermon on 'Mary, Ever Virgin, Mother of God.' {Thurian, ibid. p.76}

"I have never thought, still less taught, or declared publically, anything concerning the subject of the ever Virgin Mary, Mother of our Salvation, which could be considered dishonorable, impious, unworthy or evil... I believe with all my heart according to the word of holy gospel that this pure virgin bore for us the Son of God and that she remained, in birth and after it, a pure and unsullied virgin, for eternity." {Thurian, ibid. p.76/same sermon}.

Heinrich Bullinger's View:"Bullinger (d.1575)... defends Mary's perpetual virginity... and inveighs against the false Christians who defraud her of her rightful praise: "In Mary everything is extraordinary and all the more glorious as it has sprung from pure faith and burning love of God. 'She is the most unique and the noblest member of the Christian Community...'

John Wesley's View: (Founder of Methodism)

The Blessed Virgin Mary, who, as well after as, when she brought Him forth, continued a pure and unspotted virgin. {"Letter to a Roman Catholic"/In This Rock, Nov. 1990, p.25} Source David Armstrong: www.BiblicalCatholic.com. Please visit the website to read more. Used with permission.

13. **Comments on Martin Luther:**
    "...In the resolutions of the 95 thesis Luther rejects every blasphemy against the Virgin, and thinks that one should ask for pardon for any evil said or thought against her." (Ref: Wm. J. Cole, "Was Luther a Devotee of Mary?" In Marian Studies 1970 p.116)

"In Luther's explanation of the Magnificat in 1521, he begins and ends with an invocation of Mary, which Wright feels composed to call 'surprising' (David F. Wright, Chosen by God: Mary in Evangelical Perspective, London: Marshall Pickering, 1989, p.178, cited from Faith and Reason, spring 1994, p.6)

14. **The Power of the Rosary:** Again, before Jesus Christ's ascension into Heaven, told His apostles He has many things to say but that they will not bear them now but will send the

Holy Spirit Who will teach them, reveal what is His in John 16:12-16.

The Rosary started as a repetition of Mary's Psalter [Archangel Gabriel's and Elizabeth's greetings] in place of the 150 Psalms which corresponds to the Old Testament books of the Bible by the lay brothers in the Irish monasteries. For at that time, many of the faithful could not read so Mary's Psalter was used instead of the 150 Pslams.

When the Albigensian heresy arose about the mystery of Christ; St. Dominic asked the Blessed Virgin Mary for help. She appeared to St. Dominic with three angels and said:

"Dear Dominic, do you know which weapon the Blessed Trinity wants to use to reform the world?"

"Oh, my Lady," answered St. Dominic, "you know far better than I do because next to your Son Jesus Christ you have always been the chief instrument for our salvation."

Then Blessed Virgin Mary replied:

"I want you to know that, in this kind of warfare, the battering ram has always been the Angelic Psalter which is the foundation stone of the New Testament. Therefore if you want these hardened souls and win them over to God, preach my Psalter."

She also told him to meditate on the life of her Son to defeat the heresy.

The Blessed Virgin Mary's Psalter: The first part of it from God via Archangel Gabriel: The Angelic salutation – *"Hail Mary full of grace. The Lord is with thee."* Luke 1:28; the second part was added by Elizabeth under the influence of the Holy Spirit: *"Blessed is the fruit of thy womb."* Luke 1:42.

The last part was added in 430 A.D. to condemn the Nestorian heresy. The Council of Ephesus declared that the Blessed Virgin Mary is truly the Mother of God. This was the time she requested the last part to be added: *"Holy Mary, Mother of God, pray for us sinners, now and at the hour of our death."*

As we pray the Holy Rosary God is glorified in His most perfect creature; as our praise is directed to Mary and she passes it on to God as she did with Elizabeth in the Magnificat:

"My soul proclaims the greatness of the Lord; my spirit rejoices in God my Savior. For He has looked upon His handmaid's lowliness; behold, from now on will all ages call me blessed. The Mighty One has done great things for me, and holy is His name. His mercy is from age to age to those who fear Him. He has shown might with His arm, dispersed the arrogant of mind and heart. He has thrown down the rulers from their thrones but lifted up the lowly. The hungry He has sent away empty. He has helped Israel His servant, remembering His mercy, according to His promise to our fathers, to Abraham and to his descendants forever." Luke 1:46-55. *The Secret of the Rosary* © July 2005 by St. Louis de Montfort. Tan Book Publishers, P.O. Box 410487, Charlotte, N.C. 28241 used with permission.

The Holy Rosary is the meditation of the life, death and resurrection of our Lord and Savior Jesus Christ.

15. Testimonies on the Power of the Rosary:

The following are excerpts from the book, *Our Lady of Fatima's Peace Plan from Heaven,* Tan Books, "The Rosary is like a sword or weapon the Mother of God can use to cut down heresy and the forces of evil. It is the most powerful, and many times it has saved the world from situations as bad as, if not worse than, the one facing us today."

"Four centuries ago, the Turks were overrunning all Europe, and seemed on the verge of wiping out Christianity. When all seemed lost, Pope St. Pius V organized a great Rosary Crusade. The Christian soldiers literally went into battle with sword in one hand and rosaries in the other. On October 7, 1571, at Lepanto, one of the greatest military upsets in all history took place. The smaller Christian fleet, greatly outnumbered, defeated the mighty Turkish Armada, and Christendom was saved- all through the power of Rosary."

"In early 1964, the Country of Brazil was within days of falling into Communism. The courageous Archbishop of Rio de Janeiro broadcast radio appeals for prayer and penance in keeping with Our Lady's Fatima requests. The response of Brazilians rose and rose until it culminated in Sao Paulo on March 19. More such marches were scheduled, but on April 1, the Communists fled the country, and freedom was preserved."

"Pope Pius IX said: "Give me an army saying the Rosary, and I will conquer the world."*Our Lady of Fatima's Peace Plan From Heaven* © Tan Books & Publishers, Inc. P.O. Box 410487, Charlotte, N.C. 28241, used with permission.

Jacinta Marto, one of the children in the Fatima Apparitions was found incorrupt.

As Moses and Elijah came to Jesus Christ, spoke to Him, and strengthened Him about His crucifixion, so the Blessed Virgin Mary came to Lucy dos Santos, Francisco and Jacinta Marto to tell them what is about to happen in our world. Read about the Fatima Apparition in Portugal Newspapers: *Ilustracao,* October 29, 1917; *Ordem* or*O Dia* or the Library of Congress on the events of October 17, 1917 at Fatima, Portugal.

The Blessed Virgin Mary [BVM] appeared to St. Bernadette Soubirious at Lourdes, France, in 1854, and told her, she [the BVM] is the Immaculate Conception. St. Bernadette was found incorrupt.

16. My Observation to Substantiate the Validity that the Blessed Virgin Mary Has Influence Today.

Two articles from Pentecostal Ministers in 2007 and 2009 who wrote about the dying and what the Catholic Church was made aware of since 1935, through the Divine Mercy Chaplet and St. Faustina's visions.

The first article is by Kim Clement: Posted on www.Elijahlist.com ***An Unveiling of the Lord, High and Lifted Up*** as a subheading on January 10, 2007. *"The Spirit of God wants me to tell you that in a moment of prophecy, what took place this day with a terrorist, as he caved in realizing just before his last moment, he was getting a glimpse of the One and Only King – Christ. Every man and every woman just before they go has a glimpse of the Christ." The Spirit of God says, "Do you understand that in death, there is an unveiling of the Lord, high and lifted up? Do you understand tonight," says the Lord, "even though many reject Me, at the point of their death, there is an unveiling of the Lord God high and lifted up?"* Contact information for Kim Clement: hope@kimclement.com

The second article is by Francis Frangipane: Posted *The Silent Harvest* on September 3rd 2009 on his ministry website www.frangipane.org (It was forwarded to me in an e-mail by a friend on January 12, 2011 who did not know I was writing this.)

The Silent Harvest

"A few years ago, I had a dream in which I found myself inside the mind of a dying man. The man had been in coma for some time; his family had been praying, but they did not know whether or not he had accepted Christ. All they were sure of is that, throughout his life, he had resisted their efforts to lead him to Christ.

In the dream, I became so acutely aware of the man's state of mind that his thoughts, feelings and struggles almost seemed my own. Although his eyes were nearly closed and his vision clouded, he could see his loved ones at his bedside. I watched as he tried to reach toward his family, but outwardly his arm never lifted. Perceiving his thoughts, I heard him speak their names, but no sound whispered through his lips. A loved one holding his hands asked, "If you hear me, squeeze." He heard and pressed his fingers against hers, but no movement was seen; his hand clearly remained limp. He was conscious, he could hear their prayers, he felt the warmth of their kisses on his face, but was perfectly incapable of responding.

The pride and isolation that had, throughout his life, stood guard over his heart were gone. A physical catastrophe had taken him. Death approached, and he knew he was unprepared for eternity. Submerged beneath his motionless exterior, a war raged for his soul, which the Lord won. Subdued by the relentless force of God's love, he was finally at peace. It was during his time in the hospital that he had silently prayed and accepted Christ as his Savior. I was watching his last effort to tell them as life ebbed out of his body.

Suddenly, monitoring alarms ripped through the muffled silence of the room. His heart beat one last time and I found myself looking down at the body of a man who had just died. The room was buzzing with nurses, while his family huddled in a corner, grieving. The idea of their loved one dying without receiving Christ was more devastating than the reality of death itself. I stirred and then woke. Yet, just as I left the dream, the Lord spoke to my heart:

"Tell them he's with Me."

God is Good: Although some time has passed since I first had this dream, I am increasingly aware that many of God's people carry a deep abiding heartache concerning their loved one. Obviously, this dream does not apply to all, but there are some whom this experience is divinely directed. Thus, I submit this to you in general sense, because the Holy Spirit has assured me He will bear witness to your heart that this word is for you.

I have also felt an urgency to pass this dream to you. The Lord has important work for you. However, the enemy has used this unresolved loss to sow doubt into your soul. Not only are you troubled about your deceased loved one, but you are carrying doubts about God's love, and also the power of prayer. Your confidence in God has been compromised. Yet, it is precisely at this time that you need to stand without doubt for the other members of your family.

Beloved, though there are many questions about the mysteries of life, we must not let the unknown obscure the face of the known: God is good. We know God loves us because He sent His Son to die for our sins. Indeed, Jesus said, "He who has seen Me has seen the Father" (John 14:9). When we look at Christ, we see God, and we know that God cares.

Additionally, some of us have lost loved ones in sudden tragedies, where they seemingly had no time to repent or turn to God. Let me remind you of those who have faced near-death experiences. They tell of seeing their "life flash before [their] eyes." Indeed, they say that time itself seem to stop or move into slow motion. I believe that even in what seemed like "sudden" death, time slowed to crawl. According to their testimonies evidently, there often is enough time in this altered state to see and ponder one's entire life- and make a decision or even call upon the name of the Lord.

In spite of what we do not know about life mysteries, one thing remains eternally true: God is our loving Father. He does not desire that any should perish, and He will fight to save us, even to the moment of our death. Let us, therefore, cast our burdens upon the Lord, for he genuinely cares for us. And let us again run the endurance the race set before us, for he has promised that even for those "sitting in the …shadow of death, upon them a light dawned" (Matt. 4:16)."

The two immediate articles above showed that ***Christ is revealed to people before they die and are able to accept Him.* You will note that the Hand of God was on the Blessed Virgin Mary when she requested that *"Holy Mary Mother of God pray for us sinners now and at the hour of our death,"* be added to her Psalter and God wants her to intercede for the dying. Thus, graces are poured out for the dying to receive Christ. What Kim Clement and Francis Frangipane wrote has been revealed to the Catholic Church starting in 1935 through a Polish nun, St. Faustina.**

Below is a summary of what was revealed to St. Faustina about the dying:

"*Mercy for the Dying:* One of the greatest works of mercy we can perform- and one often overlooked- is to pray for the dying. For St. Faustina, this was an important aspect of her mission of mercy. "Oh, dying souls are in such need of prayer," St. Faustina wrote in her *Diary*. "O Jesus, inspire souls to pray often for the dying" (1015).

The Lord Himself impressed upon her the importance of such prayers when He said to her:

"Pray as much as you can for the dying. By your entreaties, obtain for them in My mercy, because they have most need of trust, and have it the least. Be assured that the grace of eternal salvation for certain souls in their final moments depends on your prayer (1777)."

"When we pray for the dying in this way, we can be assured that it opens the floodgates of Divine Mercy for souls in their time of greatest weakness and greatest need:"

"God's mercy sometimes touches the sinner at the last moment in a wondrous and mysterious way. Outwardly, it seems as if everything were lost, but it is not so. The soul, illuminated by a ray of God's power of final grace, turns to God in the last moment with such a power of love that in an instant, it receives from God forgiveness of sin and punishment…" (1698).

"The Chaplet of Divine Mercy, in 1935, St. Faustina received a vision of an angel sent before God to chastise a certain city. She began to pray for mercy, but her prayers were powerless. Suddenly she saw the Holy Trinity and felt the power of Jesus' grace within her. At the same time she found herself pleading with God for mercy with the words she heard interiorly:

"Eternal Father, I offer You the Body and Blood, Soul and Divinity of Your dearly beloved Son, Our Lord Jesus Christ, in atonement for our sins and those of the whole world; for the sake of His sorrowful Passion, have mercy on us. (Diary, 475)"

As she continued saying this inspired prayer, the angel became helpless and could not carry out the deserved punishment (see 474, 475).

The next day, as she was entering the chapel, she again heard this interior voice, instructing her how to recite the prayer that our Lord later called "the Chaplet." This time, after **have mercy on us** were added the words **and on the whole world** (476). From then on, she recited this form of prayer almost constantly, offering it especially for the dying.

In subsequent revelations, the Lord made it clear that the Chaplet was not just for her, but for the whole world. He also attached extraordinary promises to its recitation.

"Encourage souls to say the Chaplet which I have given you (1541). **Whoever will recite it will receive great mercy at the hour of death** (687). **When they say this chaplet in the presence of the dying, I stand between My Father and the dying person, not as the just Judge but as the Merciful Savior** (1541). **Priests will recommend it to sinners as their last hope of salvation. Even if there were a sinner most hardened, if he were to recite the chaplet only once, he would receive grace from My infinite mercy** (678). **I desire to grant unimaginable graces to those souls who trust in My Mercy** (678). **Through the Chaplet you will obtain everything, if what you ask for is compatible with My will** (1731)."

Another thing on praying for the dying, at the Cross the good thief a few moments before his death acknowledged Jesus Christ and Jesus told him He will be with Him in paradise. So let us not doubt the power of God as if it is not in the Bible. The whole world is not worth a single soul; our God is full of love and is full of mercy and would not allow any to perish. But it is those who know of Him and who reject Him who need repentance.

17. Divine Mercy Chaplet Novena - See Appendix A.

The Chaplet of Divine Mercy: "Prayed on ordinary rosary beads, the Chaplet of Divine Mercy is an intercessory prayer that extends the offering of the Eucharist, so it is especially appropriate to use after having the Holy Communion at Holy Mass. It may be said at any time, but our Lord specifically told St. Faustina to recite it during the nine days before the Feast of Divine Mercy (the first Sunday after Easter). He then added:

By this Novena, [of Chaplets] **I will grant every possible grace to souls** (796).

It is likewise appropriate to pray the Chaplet during the "Hour of Great Mercy" – three o'clock each afternoon (recalling the time of Christ's death on the cross). In His revelations to St. Faustina, Our Lord asked for a special remembrance of His Passion at that hour." (Diary 1320, 1572).

In summary on the Blessed Virgin Mary, in the last part of *Hail Mary it says:* ***"Holy Mary, Mother of God, Pray for Us Sinners, now and at the Hour of our death."*** With the three revelations from two Pentecostal ministers and a Polish Catholic nun it shows that Mary the Mother of Jesus Christ has a great influence still today. Her intercession draws grace from the Almighty to the sinner for salvation at the last moment before death. (**See section 33** Chaplet of Divine Mercy **Appendix A)**

To some people the Blessed Virgin Mary appeared to were found incorrupt; if her intercession stopped evil: the Turks from overrunning Europe and communism in Brazil; and salvation for men; it stands to reason that the Blessed Virgin Mary Catholics ask to intercede on their behalf and that of mankind is not evil as some people termed her. She is battling for souls not to perish. Her Son Jesus Christ told His disciples those who are not against them are for them.

Simeon said to the Blessed Virgin Mary His mother, *"Behold, this Child is destined for the fall and rise of many in Israel, and to be a sign that will be contradicted. (And you yourself a sword will pierce) so that the thoughts of many may be revealed."* Luke 1:34b-36. If anyone says that the Blessed Virgin Mary who gave birth to Jesus Christ is evil their thought has been revealed as Simeon prophesied.

On a side note, do you love your mother? Would you like someone to insult her or say she is evil? We all appreciate and study how Abraham, Moses, King David, Peter, Paul etc. obeyed God, inquired of Him, heard Him before they embarked on their mission from Him. Why do non-Catholic Christians not study the person who carried God in her womb? Some treat the Blessed Virgin Mary as if it does not matter whether or not we give her the honor due her. She carried *Jesus Christ* in her womb.

Contemplate her life from the conception of Jesus Christ to His resurrection. How life was for her and Jesus. What she must have observed and learned of Jesus Christ to tell them at the wedding in Cana, *"Whatever He tells you to do, do it!"* Nobody in the Bible has commanded such a bold confidence in God. Moses who was counted as the meekest man on earth has his failures; King David after God's heart has his failures, etc. but none on Mary except when she looked for Jesus on the way back from Jerusalem, part of her sorrows in life as prophesied by Simeon. You will say that Jesus Christ said, *"Behold Mine mother, brother, sister... those who keep the Word of God."* His intension was for us to obey Him in His word - love in all we do, no intrigue, no guile, no pride etc. He was not down playing her role in the salvation of mankind or her stand and relationship with God.

If John the Baptist said he is not worthy to carry or tie Jesus Christ's sandals. Then think about Jesus Christ's testimony of John the Baptist, *"...among those born of women there has been none greater than John the Baptist; yet the least in the Kingdom of Heaven is greater than he*. Now tell me, how we should equate with the Blessed Virgin Mary who carried Jesus Christ in the womb. She made it possible for us to be accepted in the Kingdom of Heaven? Matthew 3:11b & 11:11

In the Old Testament, the High Priest goes into the Holy of Holies to make atonement for the sins of the people with their priestly robe which has a long rope, a golden bell and a pomegranate around the hem of their garment in case they are struck dead; they will be pulled out from there, read more in Exodus 28. Uzzah was struck dead as he touched the Ark of the Covenant [see 2 Samuel 6: 1-10]. Tell me, should we not check out this person whom God has so favored that He carried God in her womb? Mary is the new Ark of the Covenant she carried Jesus Christ in her womb.

Furthermore, if John the Baptist the announcer and the baptizer of Jesus Christ was prepared from the womb as a Nazarite and he did not even marry; tell me how the person who gave birth to Jesus Christ will be prepared? In Proverbs 25:2 it says, *"It is the glory of God to conceal a matter, but it is the glory of kings to search out a matter."* NKJV. It is a mystery that was not revealed in the Scriptures how the Blessed Virgin Mary was prepared as the Mother of God. It has been revealed to some saints in the Catholic Church. She is not an ordinary woman, never was, and never will be!

There is a lot to be learned about her from what she said and did not say. John the Baptist was the Blessed Virgin Mary's nephew but he never knew who Jesus Christ was because John the Baptist testified further, saying, *"I saw the Spirit come down like a dove from the sky and remain upon Him. I did not know Him, but the One Who sent me to baptize with water told me, 'On whomever you see the Spirit come down and remain, He is the one who will baptize with the Holy Spirit. Now I have seen and testified that He is the Son of God."* John 1: 32 -34 In the passage it implied that she never opened her mouth to boast or tell relatives that she is the mother of the long awaited Messiah except those God revealed it to. In addition, the children of Israel shouted and jubilated when the Ark of the Covenant which depicts the Presence of God, is in their midst; Elizabeth rejoiced and John the Baptist in the womb leaped for joy as the Blessed Virgin Mary carried Jesus Christ [the Son of God] in the womb to visited both. Will you not leap for joy at the thought of her for what she did? She silenced the devil for mankind. The devil hates her, and that is why he subtly makes people question her so she is not given the honor that Jesus would like us to show to her.

This is what St. Maximilian Kolbe (a Catholic priest who gave his life in a Nazi Camp in order to save a Jewish man with a wife & children) said about the Blessed Virgin Mary: *"Never be afraid of loving the Blessed Virgin Mary too much. You can never love her more than Jesus did, and if anyone does not wish to have Mary Immaculate for his mother, he will not have Christ for his brother."*

Thomas a Kempis the author of *Imitations of Christ* said this about the Blessed Virgin Mary, "The devils fear your power, O Mary, and at the sound of your name they flee as from a devouring fire."

Two things to note and ponder are: the first is in the novena for the Divine Mercy chaplet Jesus Christ had revealed to St. Faustina to pray for the dying. (It was also revealed to two Pentecostal ministers that Jesus Christ appears to the dying. Kim Clement prophesied that each person before they die get a glimpse of Christ. Another Pentecostal minister, Francis Frangipane wrote about the dying being given a chance to accept Christ right before death in the "Silent Harvest." about the dying **see section 16**). The second is to be cognizant of the first, Jesus Christ would not lie to St. Faustina about the following groups of people to be prayed for in the novena:

Day 1, all mankind especially sinners;

Day 2, souls of priests & religious;

Day 3, all devout & faithful souls;

Day 4, those who do not believe in God and those who do not know Me [Jesus Christ];

Day 5, *the souls of those who have separated themselves from My Church;*

Day 6, the meek & humble souls of little children;

Day 7, the souls who especially venerate & glorify My mercy;

Day 8, souls detained in purgatory

Day 9, souls who have become lukewarm

If Jesus Christ asked for the souls in day 5 and 8 of Divine Mercy chaplet to be prayed for then it stands to reason that **purgatory is real and a need for unity is real under the Catholic Church.** The mandate that Christ gave to build His Church is to be heeded. He is a God of order; in Isaiah 40:8 it says, *"Though the grass withers, the flower wilts, the word of God stands forever."* If you think the Catholic Church is not doing some things right come join us arm yourself with what you know and let us deal with the devil together to destroy its works in God's creation.

In Hosea 6:2-3 it says, "*He will revive us after two days; on the third day He will raise us up, to live in His presence. Let us know, let us strive to know the Lord; as certain as the dawn is His coming, and judgment shines forth like the light of day! He will come to us like the rain, like spring rain that waters the earth.*"

As I reread *The Secret of the Rosary* by Louis de Monfort in October 2011, as October is the month of Our Lady of the Rosary, I unearthed some wonderful gems of wisdom:

"The Heart of My Mother has the right to be called Sorrowful and I wish this title placed before that of Immaculate because she has won it herself. The Church has defined in the case of My Mother what I Myself had ordained - her Immaculate Conception. This right which My Mother has to a title of justice is now, according to My express wish, to be known and universally accepted. She has earned it by her identification with My sorrow; by her sufferings; by her sacrifices and her immolation in Calvary endured in perfect correspondence with My grace for the salvation of mankind..." (Sept. 8, 1911)

"It is hearts that must be changed. This will be accomplished only by the Devotion proclaimed, explained, preached and recommended everywhere. Recourse to My Mother under this title I wish for her universally is the last help I shall give before the end of time." (July 2, 1940) *The Secret of the Rosary* © Louis de Montfort, Tan Books, July 2005 P.O. Box 410487, Charlotte, N.C. 28241 used with permission.

Personally, my experiences praying the Rosary have been awesome. The first time I prayed it I was ushered into the Presence of God quickly, faster than I have ever been in my life. Before, it took me about an hour of praise and worship to be overwhelmed with God's Presence.

In 2006, in a dream I gleaned that I should put the Rosary beads on my headboard due to some nightmares I was having. A second time, in a dream: to hold it in my hands. I have never had nightmares again to God's glory! One day I dreamt where a cat wanted to take a scissors from my hands but was not able to, and then I woke up. I had fallen asleep with my Rosary beads in my hands praying!

18. The Rosary: The Prayer – See section 33 Appendix B

19. Statues and Stained Glass:

In 2006 I was churning the idea in my mind regarding the statues in the sanctuary when I came across a link on the ZENIT website which is a Catholic News Agency (www.zenit.org) that wrote that statues are like a picture album. As I researched sources on Martin Luther's view of the rosary since I heard he prayed the Rosary, I came across David MacDonald's writings on www.CatholicBridge.com. I had clarity that the statues were truly a physical art form to commemorate our Christian history. Catholics do not worship the statues at all. The statues depict stories in our salvation history.

Some people may venerate a statue as they see fit but no literature I have read told me to venerate a statue, except for the Divine Mercy Image of Jesus, with rays of Blood and Water coming out from His Heart with the caption *Jesus, I Trust In You*. (You can relate this to the brazen serpent in the wilderness.)

The Divine Mercy prayer is true and powerful. I prayed it on Divine Mercy Sunday May 1, 2011 to question the validity of it, since I have been praying it since I learned about it in 2005 on a pressing issue and the prayer has not been answered. On another particular case I have prayed early in 2011 off and on. On 2011 Divine Mercy Sunday, our prayer meeting leader told us anything we ask at this hour, if it is the will of God it will be answered. Within me I said, "Lord please, answer me this week on this particular case…. to know that Divine Mercy Prayer works." I prayed it and within three hours He answered the prayer, as I learned nineteen hours later. The Divine Mercy Prayer works if it is His will and His time, I know this without a shadow of doubt.

Furthermore, the Ark of the Covenant and the Temple that King Solomon built had works of art. God endowed Bezalel, son of Uri with divine skill and understanding and knowledge in every craft, to work with cloth, precious metals, bronze and wood. There were gourds and open flowers, carved figures of cherubim, lions, palm trees, and pomegranates, [1King 6 and 7.] The children of Israel did not worship the art work in the temple. The statues and stained glass in Catholic Churches are art forms that helped the lay people of old to remember our salvation history and Bible stories. Besides, one retains more from visuals than written form. Thus, they were able to remember and retain the Bible stories they were told. It also serves to beautify the Sanctuary; our God is a God of beauty.

I have been fully convinced that God is not against having a form of art in the Sanctuary. The flowers people use today to decorate the Sanctuary I believe are not an object of worship. David MacDonald said something in his website that is so true: *"If Catholics worship idols then those who watch Jesus film, Christian film or biblical film are worshipping idols."* (www.CatholicBridge.com) Used with permission.

As I finished the final editing of this book, I was asked why Catholics still leave Christ on the cross. I replied it has power, as simply as I have experienced it. Later, I found out on the internet, and few weeks later at a homily during Mass that it was based on 1 Corinthians 1:23-24, "But we proclaim Christ crucified, [a stumbling block to the Jews and foolishness to the Gentiles, but to those who are called, Jews and Greeks alike,] Christ the power of God and the wisdom of God." Note worthy is a statement I read in Wikipedia about exorcist Gabriele Amorth, who "Stated that the crucifix is one of the most effective means of averting or opposing demons; it is believed to ward off vampires, incubi, succubi, and other evils."

Personally I will ask a question, "Will one be worshipping an idol with the Nativity Scene in their court yard or home?" Saint Francis of Assisi was the first person to start a live Nativity Scene that evolved to the ornamental decorative ones today. What the Nativity Scene reminds us of is stirring up the anti-Christ spirit in the society; that is why in some places people want to it removed from the public square!

Finally, Galatians 3: 1 "O stupid Galatians! Who has bewitched you, before whose eyes Jesus Christ was publicly portrayed as crucified?" There must have been an image depicting Jesus Christ crucified in use by the early Christians!

20. Stations of the Cross:

The fourteen Stations of the Cross commemorate the stages Jesus Christ went through from the Garden of Gethsemane, to the tomb and give Him due respect and honor for the sufferings He went through for us. Tremendous grace is poured out during Lent, on Fridays or any time, as you pray and meditate the Passion of our Lord. When you remember His sufferings one will not have the heart and mind to backslide. The children of Israel were told to build booths to remember the time they were in the wilderness on their way to the Promised Land. They were told to commemorate the Passover; consequently, it is in order to have Stations of the Cross inside the Sanctuary.

I will share a part of Eileen Fisher's e-mail to me on Wednesday March 16, 2011 that has some parts of the Stations of the Cross and the Rosary (we do not know each other personally; her name was laid in my heart in 2009. I searched her name in the Google search engine saw her website, visited and left my email address. Since then I have been on her ministry's e-mail list for corporate prophetic word) this is the prophetic corporate word on March 8, 2011: ***"Behold Me on the Cross, Behold Me in the tomb. Behold Me in the Resurrection. Behold Me upon the Throne…"*** She is a non-Catholic Christian, and additional information may be found on her website: www.eileenfisher.org.

21. Martin Luther removed the portions of the Bible that contradicted his teachings.

(i) Old Testament: 1 & 2 Macabbees, Tobit, Sirach, Wisdom, Baruch, Judith.

The discovery of the Dead Sea Scrolls in 1947 confirmed some of the 7 Old Testament books Martin Luther removed. Points from **sections 22 to 24** below explained just few points in the teachings contained in the books. Check the teachings, the revelations by the two Pentecostal ministers and St. Faustina, a Catholic nun about the dying, the Scripture in Peter about Jesus Christ visiting the spirit in prison, the institution of Hanukkah to confirm if the books should be removed or not.

Maccabbees is an excellent account of how the bravery of Judas Maccabbee the third son of Mattathias, and his brothers led the revolt against the Seleucid kings who persecuted the Jews. To celebrate the victory Hanukkah was instituted – Feast of the Dedication [Eight-day Festival of Lights]. Jesus Christ was at the temple area as mentioned in John 10:22-23. It was to celebrate the Maccabbees' rededication of the altar and re-consecration of the temple in 164 B.C., after their desecration by Anticochus IV Epiphanes.

Thus, the people and the Temple were preserved in order to usher in Christ for our salvation. It is a bridge of Jewish history between the Old Testament foreign occupation of the land of Israel and the New Testament foreign occupation of the land. Reflect on the Old Testament and all of a sudden you see Roman soldiers in the New Testament, in the entire Bible (non-Catholic Bible) you never read about how they came. How and when did they get there in the first place? If you read Maccabbees it will tell you how and when the Jews and Romans started dealing with each other.

Judas Maccabbee had victory against all odds by his prayer based on vision given to him. The vision given to him, was that a former high priest was praying with outstretched arms for the whole Jewish community; who relates that Jeremiah the prophet loves and prays for his people and their holy city. Jeremiah presented a gold sword to Judas, a gift from God to crush his enemies.

Also in Maccabbees, it has a moving account of a woman with her seven sons who refused to defile themselves and were martyred for their faith. See **Appendix E.**

When you read the Maccabbees you will understand and appreciate the social, cultural and political dynamics of the time and how God used these forces to fulfill the Old Testament prophecies in the New Testament.

The Book of Tobit, written before the New Testament, has the following portion similar to Revelation 21:10-21

Tobit 13:16b – 18a *"The gates of Jerusalem shall be built with sapphire and emerald, and all your walls with precious stones. The towers of Jerusalem shall be built with gold, and their battlement with pure gold. The streets of Jerusalem shall be paved with rubies and stones of Ophir; the gates of Jerusalem shall sing hymns of gladness, and all her houses shall cry out, "Alleluia!"*

The Book of Sirach is an excellent source of moral education especially for children and youth. In Sirach 12:19 *"When he says: 'I have found rest, now I will feast on my possessions,' he does not know how long it will be till he dies and leaves them to others."* This is similar to the parable of the rich man in Luke 12:19-21. Jesus may have read it or He is referring to it.

The Book of Wisdom speaks for itself. Here is a sentence in the preface to the *Book of Wisdom*, "The first ten chapters especially form a preparation for the fuller teachings of Christ and His Church."

The Book of Baruch, do you remember Jeremiah's scribe in Jeremiah 36:4-32? Do you think that the book then is to be discarded? You be the judge.

The Book of Judith is about how a Jewish widow delivered the Jews from the hand of their enemies. You know that throughout history to this present moment the enemy of our Lord is still fighting the Jews using human beings.

Please try and read these wonderful books for they are missing. They will refresh your soul, renew your mind and warm your heart to the things of God.

(ii) New Testament: Hebrews, James, Jude, and Revelations, were removed later and were put back by Protestants scholars.

It is quite remarkable in Hebrews Chapter 11 listed the great heroes and heroines of faith from Abel in verse 4 to the account of Shadrach, Meshach, and Abed-Nego in verse 34b. However, Hebrews 11 verses 34b to 38 you will notice that these unnamed heroes and heroines what they did you cannot find the account in the Old Testament of the non-Catholic Bible. Hebrews 11:34b to 38 recalls what took place in 1 & 2 Maccbees and Judith.

Here is a comparative analysis: Hebrews 11:34b "Out of weakness they were made powerful, became strong in battle, and turned back foreign invaders Judith turned back the invading forces of Holofernes, general-in-chief of King Nebuchadnezzar army.

Hebrews 11:35 "Women received back their dead through resurrection. Some were tortured and would not accept deliverance, in order to obtain a better resurrection." 2 Maccabees 6:18 to 7:41 fits perfectly with this verse, read it in **Appendix E.**

Hebrews 11:36 "Others endured mockery, scourging, even chains and imprisonment." 2 Maccabees reads "…I am not only enduring terrible pain in my body from scourging, but suffering it with joy in my soul because of my devotion to Him."

Hebrews 11:37b "…sawed in two, put to death at sword's point; they went about in skins of sheep or goats, needy, afflicted, tormented." 1 Maccabees 1:60-63 "Women who had had their children circumcised were put to death, in keeping with the decree, with babies hung from their necks; their families also and those who had circumcised them were killed. But many in Israel were determined and resolved in their hearts not to eat anything unclean; they preferred to die rather than to be defiled with unclean food or profane the holy covenant; and they did die. Terrible affliction was upon Israel."

Hebrews 11:38 "The world was not worthy of them. They wandered about in deserts and mountains, in caves and in crevices in the earth." Similar to 1 Maccabees 2:28-30 "There upon he fled to the mountains with his sons, leaving behind in the city all their possessions. Many who sought to live according to righteous and religious custom went out into the desert to settle there, they and their sons, their wives, and their cattle, because misfortunes pressed so hard on them. [Cross reference in 2 Maccabees 5:27 "But Judas Maccabeus with about nine others withdrew to the wilderness where he and his companions lived like wild animals in hills, continuing to eat what grew wild to avoid sharing the defilement."] 2 Maccabees 6:11 "Others, who had assembled in nearby caves to observe the Sabbath in secret, were betrayed to Philip and all burned to death. In their respect for the holiness of that day, they had scruples about defending themselves."

22. **Asking the Saints to Pray for us:** In 2 Maccabees 15:12-16 for details of the Scriptures **See Appendix C.**

In Maccabees it mentioned that Onias (saint) a former Jewish high priest was praying for the Jewish community at the time they were being oppressed. The Jews had victory over a host of well equipped army. Some Christians do not know this part of their spiritual heritage.

It is not necromancy to ask the saints to pray for us. It is like asking a friend to pray for you. Remember Jesus said Abraham is not dead but living. Why did Moses and Elijah come to Jesus Christ at the Mount of Transfiguration? There was an exchange that pertained to Christ's crucifixion and resurrection, because He told Peter, James and John not to tell anyone what they saw till His glorification.

In Hebrews 12:1 the author tells us, *"Therefore, since we are surrounded by so* ***great a cloud of witnesses,*** *let us rid ourselves of every burden and sin that clings to us and persevere in running the race that lies before us."* The cloud of witnesses, are the saints that cheer and support us through prayers.

In September 6, entry of the Devotional ***GOD CALLING by Two Listeners,*** **Edited by A.J. Russell:**

"Your loved ones are very safe in My Keeping. Learning and loving and working, theirs is a life of happiness and progress. They live to serve, and serve they truly do. They serve Me and those they love. Ceaselessly they serve.

But their ministrations, so many, so diverse, you see no more than those in My time on earth in human form could have seen the angles who ministered unto Me in the wilderness.

How often mortals rush to earthly friends who can serve them in so limited a way, when the friends who are free from the limitations of humanity can serve them so much better, understand better, protect better, plan better, and even plead better their cause with Me.

You do well to remember your friends in the Unseen. Companying with them the more you live in this Unseen World the gentler will be your passing when it comes. Earth's troubles and difficulties will seem, even now, less overwhelming as you look, not at the things that are seen but at the real, Eternal Life.

"And this is Life Eternal that we may know Thee, the Only True God, and Jesus Christ whom Thou hast sent."

Learning to know Me draws that Kingdom very near, and in Me, and through Knowledge of Me, the dear ones there become *very* near and dear."

23. **Praying for the Souls of the Dead:** 2 Maccabbees 12:43-46 for details of this Scripture **see Appendix D.**

Jesus Christ told St. Faustina a Polish nun to visit purgatory and pray for souls there. **See section 24** on purgatory below and Divine Mercy Chaplet Day Eight, **see Appendix A**

Jesus Christ visited souls in prison: 1 Peter 3: 18-20 *"For Christ also suffered for sins once, the righteous for the sake of the unrighteousness, that He might lead you to God. Put to death in the flesh, He was brought to life in the spirit. In it He also went to preach to the spirits in prison. Who had once been disobedient while God patiently waited in the days of Noah during the building of the ark, in which a few persons, eight in all, were saved through water."* See the Purgatory **section 24** below. This is to validate praying for the dead.

Furthermore in 1 Corinthians 2:15 it says, *"But if someone's work is burned up, that one will suffer loss; the person will be saved, but only as through fire."* Is it in heaven will someone's work suffer loss? Nor is it in hell can someone be saved? So it must be purgatory that one's work can suffer loss but the person be saved through fire!

24. **Purgatory:** Here is an excerpt from the Divine Mercy Message, "Jesus Himself encouraged St. Faustina to remember the souls in purgatory. He told her: "Enter purgatory often, because the [souls] need you there." (Diary, 1738). See the Divine Mercy Chaplet **see Appendix A**.

See Bible texts in 1 Peter 3:18-20, and 1 Corinthians 3: 14 &15, also in **section 23** above for evidence of souls in purgatory.

The Catechism of the Catholic Church teaches: "All who die in God's grace and friendship, but still imperctly purified, are indeed assured of their eternal salvation; but after death they undergo purification, so as to achieve the holiness necessary to enter the joy of heaven." (1030)*Diary of St. Faustina Kowalska: Divine Mercy in My Soul* © 1987 Marian Fathers of the Immaculate Conception, Stockbridge, MA 02163. Used with permission.

25. **Relics:** The bones of Elisha raised a dead man. Handkerchiefs that touched Paul's body cured the sick. Likewise, the relics of Catholic saints have worked miracles too (some saints have been found incorrupt.)

26. **Confession:** The Institution of Sacrament of Reconciliation – Confession; you find it in John 20:21-23 *"Jesus said to them again, 'Peace be with you. As the Father has sent Me, so I send you.' And when He had said this, He breathed on them and said to them, 'Receive the Holy Spirit. Whose sins you forgive are forgiven them, and whose sins you retain are retained.'"*

In the above Scripture passage Christ **Instituted the Sacrament of Reconciliation** what is commonly called Confession. It is a sign of humility and obedience to His command. As I heard from a priest, "It is the best psychological therapy free of charge." Truly it is, you feel like flying after a good confession. It is blissful.

It is confirmed in James 5:16 *"Therefore, confess your sins to one another and pray for one another, that you may be healed. The fervent prayer of a righteous person is very powerful."*

One thing I will mention is that in the Law of Moses when people sinned they were required to go to the priests to offer their sin offerings. It must be a shadow of confession.

27. Priests not Marrying:

There were men in the Bible who did not marry - Daniel, Elijah, Elisha, Jeremiah, Paul, Barnabas, John the Beloved, and John the Baptist.

In Matt. 19:10-12 "*His [Jesus Christ] disciples said to Him, 'If that is the case of a man with his wife, it is better not to marry.' He answered, 'Not all can accept this word, but only those to whom that is granted. Some are incapable of marriage because they were born so, some, because they were made so by others, some because they have renounced marriage for the kingdom of heaven. Whoever can accept this ought to accept it.'*"

Then in 1 Corinthians 7:7 Paul advised them thus, "*Indeed, I wish everyone to be as I am, but each has a particular gift from God, one of one kind and one another.*"

In 1 Corinthians 7:32-33 Paul states, "*I should like you to be free of anxieties. An unmarried man is anxious about the things of the Lord, how he may please the Lord. But a married man is anxious about the things of the world, how he may please his wife, and he is divided.*

Catholic priests used to be married but at the Council of Trent (1545 -1563) it was changed and has become Church law. This is only in the Latin rite but in the Eastern rite the priests marry. It is now a discipline as a celibate vocation. Celibacy is for those who want to serve without distractions. It is to imitate Christ theologically; and practically to be able to focus on one family. It may or it may not change. But ministers of God from other Christian denominations who have come back to Catholic Church still retain their marriage and serve God as His priests.

It is noteworthy that priests in the Old Testament come to minister stayed in the temple from beginning to the end of their shift no matter the number of days they were assigned. You know what? Catholic priests offer Mass daily except for Good Friday.

There are some priests who have erred or broken their vow of chastity. Some have done atrocious things. We pray for them, instead of pointing fingers, so the devil does not infiltrate their ranks. As Jesus Christ said, *"Let the one among you who is without sin be the first to throw a stone..."* [John 8:7]

28. On Women not Ordained as Priests.

In the Old Testament women were not in line for the Priestly Office, and in the New Testament Jesus Christ selected none as one of the twelve apostles. However, women were mightily used of God from Sarah to the Blessed Virgin Mary. God has roles for each; if we all do what we are called to do faithfully; we all will radiate God's glory. If you are a woman and you believe God called you to preach, prophecy, go ahead: there is print, radio, TV, cable, internet, and the latest media yet to be discovered. But did He call you to be ordained as a priest? I do not know; there were none in the Bible; women led men to war but in the Temple we were not told that they officiated as priests. We see the aged Prophetess Anna in the Temple worshipping and praying to God day and night without leaving the Temple having been widowed after seven years of marriage.

There are women God chose and some women who chose on their own to serve God without distraction down through Church history that have influenced humanity and the world history without being a priest.

Today, it still holds in the Catholic Church. Not only singles, but, also, married women serve God faithfully in the various capacities there are abbess of convents, theologians, teachers, professors, writers, Eucharist ministers, lectors, catechists, choristers, caregivers for the poor etc.

There are several examples in modern history of single and married women who served God out of their own free will and have impacted humanity and our world. St. Catherine of Siena, St. Teresa of Avila, Blessed Mother Teresa, Dorothy Day. Mother Angelica, a media magnate is serving God quietly in Irondale, Alabama today. There are countless other Catholic women who are serving God with their time, talent and treasure without being a priest. They have been given full rein and support from the Church leadership.

Thus, the above is my observation; the final word is from the Lord, not man!

29. On Suffering and Poverty:

Suffering - Some think that the Catholic Church teaches that one should live a life of suffering and not to pray when one is sick; that is not so. The Catholic Church teaches that if we suffer or are sick we should pray. We pray and let the will of the Lord be done. We believe we may be healed but if we are not healed, we offer the sufferings or pain to God for the salvation of others. Paul in one of his Epistles told us he had a thorn in the flesh and he asked God to remove it and the Lord told him His grace is sufficient for him.

In Colossians 1:24 it says, *"Now I rejoice in my sufferings for your sake, and my flesh I am filling up what is lacking in the afflictions of Christ on behalf of His body, which is the Church."*

In Hebrews 5:8-9 it says, *"Son though He was, He learned obedience from what He suffered; and when He was made perfect, He became the source of eternal salvation for all who obey Him."*

Furthermore, in 1 Peter 4:19 it says, *"As a result, those who suffer in accord with God's will hand over their souls over to a faithful creator as they do good."*

Suffering is a cross we did not choose but God arranged that we may conform to the image of His Son. As each face is different so is each cross. It is the power of God at work in us. No cross, no glory. As Romans 8:18-19 states, *"I consider that the sufferings of this present time are as nothing compared with the glory to be revealed for us. For creation awaits with eager expectation the revelation of the children of God."* For more on suffering read 2 Corinthians 1:4-10.

Poverty - Religious priests take a vow of chastity, obedience and poverty. Whatever money they earn from their work or family inheritance they use for their community, the needy or the poor, not for themselves as personal property. But the diocesan priests do not take a vow of poverty.

Throughout history some wealthy Catholics have given up their wealth to serve Christ and His Church by becoming monks, priests or religious. The priests and religious take a vow of chastity, live on a small salary, thus, leading to a life of simplicity. St. Francis of Assisi was one of them.

The lay people are never encouraged to be poor, but to use their money to serve those who are less privileged. Remember it was the Catholics that started Universities, hospitals and hospices. As 3 John 2 says, *"Beloved, I hope you are prospering in every respect and are in good health, just as your soul is prospering."*

Besides, monks, religious priests, and women religious chose a simple life so as to serve God with sincerity of heart. With focus on the sheep: through parishes, monasteries, schools, hospitals, and serving the poor. (They vow to live a simple life of obedience, chastity, poverty, humility and love.) Very, very, very few have taken Church money for personal gain. Some write books or give talks, and the money earned is used for the poor or some needy in the society or a cause they believe in. They do not even have personal retirement funds. They depend on the charity of the diocese, family or friends to live on after they retire. They live a simple life to serve God.

Catholic priests choose a life of simplicity so as to serve Christ and His Church, but they do not teach the laity to be financially poor. There are some Catholic millionaires and billionaires who have given great amount of their money for the cause of Christ and humanity quietly. The Church did not tell them to be financially poor or to renounce their wealth. People who do, do it out of their own conviction and conscience.

30. Prejudice and Racism:

The demon of prejudice and racism should be dealt with. It starts from the heart and the mind. It is perpetuated by the human ego and the society. We should develop programs that will root it out from our midst. Parents develop strategies to stop sibling rivalry among their children. In the early Church ethnicity came up between Jewish Christians and Hellenic Christians; the apostles chose men to take care of the problem; thus, the institution of deacons began. Paul in his Epistles sorted it out.

Let not the society and the government dictate to us how we should treat our brethren. In the Scriptures when Paul was being sought after to be killed, it was the brethren that lowered him in a basket and let him through the window to another city. We should not team with society and oppress the brethren. In the history of some societies this has been done and God did not appreciate it.

In a devotional *God Calling by Two Listeners* edited by A.J. Russell, I quote, "**Second Advent, November 5** entry: *Jesus, Comforter of all the sorrowing, help us to bring Thy comfort into every heart and life to which Thou art longing to express that comfort through us. Use us, Lord. The years may be many or few. Place us where we can best serve Thee, and influence most for Thee.* The world would be brought to Me so soon, so soon, if only all who acknowledge Me as Lord, as Christ, gave themselves unreservedly to be used by Me.

I could use *each* human body as mightily as I used My own human body as a channel for Divine Love and power. I do not delay My second coming. My *followers* delay it. If each lived for Me, by Me, allowing Me to live in him, to use him to express the Divine through him, as I expressed it when on earth, then long ago the world would have been drawn to Me, and I should have come to claim My own. So seek, My children, to live, knowing no other desire but to express Me, and show My Love to your world."

The culture Jesus, Mary, Joseph, the apostles, and disciples lived in, was one of inclusiveness as one family. All belong; there are no second class citizens. It is expressed well in Psalm 133 – *"Behold how good and how pleasant is the dwelling of brothers, moreover, in unity. Like the precious oil upon the head running down upon the beard, the beard of Aaron, running down over his garments. Like the dew of Hermon descending upon the mountains of Zion, for there the Lord has commanded blessings. May there be life forever!"* New King James Version

We the Church should teach and practice the way things should be done, and how people are treated. It was because of the way the believers in Antioch treated one another that they were called Christians – little Christ or Christ likeness. We look out for each other, not how we will outwit one another or treat another to show that my race is better than your race.

In Zechariah 7:9-10 it reminds us concerning our hearts towards others, *"Thus says the Lord of Hosts, Render true judgment, and show kindness and compassion toward each other. Do not oppress the widow or the orphan, the alien or the poor; do not plot evil against one another in your hearts."*

We are cautioned in Psalm 62: 12-13, *"One thing God has said; two things I have heard: Power belongs to God; so too, Lord, does kindness, and You render to each of us according to our deeds."*

2 Corinthians 5:10 further admonishes us, *"For we must all appear before the judgment seat of Christ, so that each one may receive recompense, according to what he did in the body, whether good or evil."*

Finally, Revelations 22:12 affirm the above Scriptures, *"Behold, I Am coming soon, I bring with Me the recompense I will give to each according to his deeds."*

Consider the examples in the Acts of the Apostles; these are lives lived of baptized believers empowered by the Holy Spirit to establish the Kingdom of God here on earth. The baton is now in our hands in this generation. The Epistles offer corrections for our sinful nature, encouraging us to abide in Christ and in Him alone. If it is hard for you to accept other races, socioeconomic groups etc. ask God for mercy and grace to do so.

Another thing to ponder: "If you do not accept a Christian brother here on earth, where are you heading? The brother is heading to heaven. Thus, do not eliminate yourself. If you cannot stand him as a brother here; you cannot stand him in heaven." So treat a brother as you want to be treated!

Please pray that the power of racism and prejudice together with religious spirit, political spirit, control spirit and self-ambition in the Body of Christ to be broken. Pray for your local assembly and the Body of Christ universal to worship God in spirit and in truth. Let His people experience true liberty...righteousness, joy and peace in the Holy Spirit!

Please note that not all Christian leaders and Christian laity are prejudiced or racist.

31. Summary

With all the points listed above. The order of worship service in the church as Justin the Martyr 66- 67 AD explained in his Apology 1; which is still the order of Mass in the Catholic Church today; the evidence of the real Presence of Jesus Christ in the Eucharist, the Incorruptibles, the Miracles of the Eucharist, the appearance of Jesus Christ before the dying as revealed to St. Faustina in 1935, to Kim Clement in 2007 & Francis Frangipane in 2009.

A striking observation, the list of people to be included in the Divine Mercy Chaplet: on the fifth day: *The souls of those who have separated themselves from My Church, and immerse them in the ocean of My mercy. During My bitter Passion they tore at My Body and Heart, that is, My Church. As they return to unity with the Church My wounds heal and in this way they alleviate My Passion.* Then on the eighth day: The souls in purgatory. Also, the Divine Mercy Chaplet has Hail Mary in it, the evidence in the power of the Rosary, with cognizance of John 17:20- 26. I believe it is now for us to go to God in prayer with open heart and mind to hear and know what the Lord is saying to His Church and to do what He says by His special grace.

As I was rounding up on this book, I was reminded of the reading for September 11, 2011 Catholic Mass readings and what happened on that day ten years ago in the United States of America September 11, 2001. The readings are arranged in advance so that the whole Bible is read in three year periods at Mass (Year A, B, & C). My inherited New St. Joseph Sunday Missal has it planned from 1998 to 2016 with Bible texts being assigned for each Sunday.

Sunday, 9-11-11, the 10th Anniversary of 9/11 was on Forgiveness. The 1st Reading taken from Sirach 27:30-28:9 the need for forgiveness; Responsorial taken from Psalm 103 God's mercy; 2nd Reading taken from Romans 14:7-9 God's partner; Gospel acclamation taken from John 13:34 love one another, and the Gospel of Mathew 18:21-35 forgiving our neighbor. This was read in all the Catholic parishes in the United States of America.

For the benefit of those who do not have Catholic Bible I will quote Sircah 27:30-28:9 *"Wrath and anger are hateful things, yet the sinner hugs them tight. The vengeful will suffer the Lord's vengeance, for He remembers their sins in detail. Forgive your neighbor's injustice; then when you pray, your own sins will be forgiven. Could anyone nourish anger against another and expect healing from the Lord? Could anyone refuse mercy to another like himself, can he seek pardon for his own sins? If one who is but flesh cherish wrath who will forgive his sins? Set enmity aside."*

To the glory of God Who by the power of the Holy Spirit guided the people in putting the Liturgy of the Word for the day, I will quote Romans 14:7-9 *"Brothers and sisters: None of us lives for oneself. For if we live, we live for the Lord, and if we die, we die for the Lord; so then, whether we live or die, we are the Lord's. For this is why Christ died and came to life, that He might be Lord of both the dead and the living."* This passage gives one the comfort to know all the souls that died in the attack are in God's Hands; and at the same time it will heal the souls of those who lost loved ones who may still be grieving inwardly.

So my brothers and sisters in Christ, God speaks to us in different ways if we open our heart and mind to listen. He has spoken in these passages read at Mass on this day 9-11-11. I believe you will choose what our great and good Lord has requested of us all, to be one, so that the world may know that He has sent Jesus Christ in the world to save us, thereby the unbelievers will come to believe.

32. What Jesus Christ said and prayed. God's response to your response to unity.

Jesus Christ prayed in John 17:20-21 *"I pray not only for them, but also for those who will believe in Me through their word, so that they may all be one, as You, Father, are in Me and I in You, that they also may be in us, that the world may believe that You sent Me.*

By God's special grace may He say to each one of us on that Day!

"...Well done, My good and faithful servant. Since you were faithful in small matters, I will give you great responsibilities. Come and share your master's joy." Matt.:25:23

May the Lord not say the following Scripture below to any of one us:

"Not everyone that says to me Lord, Lord, will enter the kingdom of My Father in heaven; many will say to Me on that day, 'Lord, Lord, did we not prophesy in Your name? Did we not drive out demons in Your name? Then I will declare to them solemnly, 'I never knew you. Depart from Me, you evildoers." Matt.:7:21-23

May He give each the grace to act as the following Scripture says, *"If you keep My commandments, you will remain in My love, just as I have kept My Father's commandments and remain in His love. I have told you this so that My joy might be in you and your joy might be complete. This is My commandment: love one another as I love you."* John 15: 9-12

Though God does not compel us to go against our will as a song writer wrote.

I will end with a quote from a Jewish prayer book: *"A man forever should be God-fearing in the innermost recesses of his heart, acknowledge the truth, and speak the truth in his heart."* Siddur Tehilla HASHEM, Nusach Ha-Ari- Zal 5748-1988 © MerkosL'InyoneiChinuch, Inc. Brooklyn, NY 11213

33. Appendix A to E

Appendix A

How to recite the Chaplet of Divine Mercy: (On ordinary rosary beads) (Diary, 476)

The Our Father

"Our Father, Who art in heaven, hallowed be Thy name; Thy kingdom come; Thy will be done, on earth as it is in heaven. Give us this day our daily bread; and forgive us our trespasses as we forgive those who trespass against us; and lead us not into temptation, but deliver us from the evil." Matthew 6:9-13

The Hail Mary

Hail Mary full of grace, the Lord is with you. Blessed are you among women, and blessed is the fruit of thy womb, Jesus. Holy Mary, Mother of God, pray for us sinners now and at the hour of our death.

The Apostles' Creed

On the Large Bead before Each Decade: Eternal Father, I offer You the Body and Blood, Soul and Divinity of Your dearly beloved Son, Our Lord Jesus Christ, in atonement for our sins and those of the whole world.

On the 10 Beads of Each Decade: For the sake of His sorrowful passion, have mercy on us and on the whole world.

Concluding Doxology: (after five decades) Holy God, Holy Mighty One, Holy Immortal One, have mercy on us and on the whole world. **(Three times)**

Optional Concluding Prayer: Eternal God, in whom mercy is endless and the treasury of compassion inexhaustible, look kindly upon us and increase Your mercy in us, that in difficult moments we might not despair nor become despondent, but with great confidence submit ourselves to Your holy will, which is Love and Mercy itself (950).

Prayers for the Novena: (Diary, 1209-1229) Novena intentions and the Chaplet of Divine Mercy prayers immediately above are said together.

First Day: Today bring to Me – All Mankind, Especially All Sinners, and immerse them in the ocean of My mercy. In this way you will console Me in the bitter grief into which the loss of souls plunges Me.

Most Merciful Jesus, whose very nature it is to have compassion on us and to forgive us, do not look upon our sins but upon our trust which we place in Your infinite goodness. Receive us all into the abode of Your Most compassionate Heart, and never let us escape from it. We beg this of You by Your love which unites You to the Father and the Holy Spirit.

Eternal Father, turn Your merciful gaze upon all mankind and especially upon poor sinners, all enfolded in the Most Compassionate Heart of Jesus. For the sake of His sorrowful Passion show us Your mercy, that we may praise the omnipotence of Your mercy. Amen.

Second Day: Today bring to Me – The Souls of Priests And Religious,

and immerse them in My unfathomable mercy. It was they who gave Me strength to endure My bitter Passion. Through them as through channels My mercy flows out upon mankind.

Most Merciful Jesus, from whom comes all that is good, increase Your grace in men and women consecrated to Your service, that they may perform worthy works of mercy; and that all who see them may glorify the Father of mercy who is in heaven.

Eternal Father, turn Your merciful gaze upon the company of chosen ones in Your vineyard – upon the souls of priests and religious; and endow them with the strength of Your blessing. For the love of the Heart of Your Son in which they are enfolded, impart to them Your power and light, that they may be able to guide others in the way of salvation and with one voice sing praise to Your boundless mercy for ages without end. Amen.

Third Day: Today bring to Me – All Devout And Faithful Souls,

and immerse them in the ocean of My mercy. These souls brought Me consolation on the Way of the Cross. They were that drop of consolation in the midst of an ocean of bitterness.

Most merciful Jesus, from the treasury of Your mercy, You impart Your graces in great abundance to each and all. Receive us into the abode of Your most compassionate Heart and never let us escape from it. We beg this grace of You by that most wondrous love for the heavenly Father with which Your Heart burns so fiercely.

Eternal Father, turn Your merciful gaze upon faithful souls, as upon the inheritance of Your Son. For the sake of His sorrowful Passion, grant them Your blessing and surround them with Your constant protection. Thus may they never fail in love or lose the treasury of the holy faith, but rather, with all the hosts of Angels and Saints, may they glorify Your boundless mercy for endless ages. Amen.

Fourth Day: Today bring to Me - Those Who do not Believe in God And Those Who do not yet Know Me.

I was thinking also of them during My bitter Passion, and their future zeal comforted My Heart. Immerse them in the ocean of My mercy.

Most compassionate Jesus, You are the Light of the whole world. Receive into Your most compassionate Heart the souls of those who do not believe in God and of those who as yet do not know You. Let the rays of Your grace enlighten them that they, too, together with us, may extol Your wonderful mercy; and do not let them escape from the abode which is Your Most Compassionate Heart

Eternal Father, turn Your merciful gaze upon the souls of those who do not know You, but who are enclosed in the Most Compassionate Heart of Jesus. Draw them to the light of the Gospel. These souls do not know what great happiness it is to love You. Grant that they, too, may extol the generosity of Your mercy for endless ages. Amen.

Fifth Day: Today bring to Me- The Souls of those Who have Separated Themselves From My Church,

and immerse them in the ocean of My mercy. During My bitter Passion they tore at My Body and Heart, that is, My Church. As they return to unity with the Church My wounds heal and in that way they alleviate My Passion.

Most merciful Jesus, goodness itself, You do not refuse light to those who seek it of You. Receive into the abode of Your most compassionate Heart the souls of those who have separated themselves from Your Church. Draw them by Your light into the unity of the Church, and do not let them escape from the abode of Your Most Compassionate Heart; but bring it that they, too, come to glorify the generosity of Your mercy.

Eternal Father, turn Your merciful gaze upon the souls of those who have squandered Your blessings and misused Your graces by obstinately persisting in their errors. Do not look upon their errors, but upon the love of Your own Son and upon His bitter Passion, which He underwent for their sake, since they, too, are enclosed in His Most compassionate Heart. Bring it about that they also may glorify Your great mercy for endless ages. Amen.

Sixth Day: Today bring to Me – The Meek And Humble Souls And the Souls of Little Children,

and immerse them in My mercy. These souls most closely resemble My Heart. They strengthened Me during My bitter agony. I saw them as earthly Angels, who will keep vigil at My altars. I pour out upon them torrents of grace. Only the humble soul is capable of receiving My grace. I favor humble souls with My confidence.

Most merciful Jesus, You yourself have said, "Learn from Me for I am meek and humble of heart." Receive into the abode of Your Heart all meek and humble souls and the souls of little children. These souls send all heaven into ecstasy and they are the heavenly Father's favorites. They are a sweet-smelling bouquet before the throne of God; God himself takes delight in their fragrance. These souls have permanent abode in Your most compassionate Heart, O Jesus, and they unceasingly sing out a hymn of love and mercy.

Eternal Father, turn Your merciful gaze upon meek souls, upon humble souls, and upon little children who are enfolded in the abode which is the Most Compassionate Heart of Jesus. These souls bear closest resemblance to Your Son. Their fragrance rises from earth and reaches Your very throne. Father of mercy and of all goodness, I beg You by the love You bear these souls and by the delight You take in them: Bless the whole world, that all souls together may sing out praises of Your mercy for endless ages. Amen.

Seventh Day: Today bring to Me- The Souls Who especially Venerate And Glorify My Mercy,

and immerse them in My mercy. These souls sorrowed most over my Passion and entered most deeply into My spirit. They are living images of My Compassionate Heart. These souls will shine with special brightness in the next life. Not one of them will go into the fire of hell. I shall particularly defend each one of them at the hour of death.

Most merciful Jesus, whose Heart is Love Itself, receive into the abode of Your most compassionate Heart the souls of those who particularly extol and venerate the greatness of Your mercy. These souls are mighty with the very power of God Himself. In the midst of all afflictions and adversities they go forward, confident of Your mercy; and united to You, O Jesus, they carry all mankind on their shoulders. These souls will not be judged severely, but Your mercy will embrace them as they depart from this life.

Eternal Father, turn Your merciful gaze upon souls who glorify and venerate Your greatest attribute, that of Your fathomless mercy, and who are enclosed in the Most Compassionate Heart of Jesus. These souls are a living Gospel; their hands are full of deeds of mercy, and their hearts, overflowing with joy, sing out a canticle of mercy to You, O Most High! I beg You O God: Show them Your mercy according to the hope and trust they have placed in You. Let there be accomplished in them the promise of Jesus, who said to them that during their life, but especially at the hour of death, the souls who will venerate this fathomless mercy of His, He, Himself, will defend as His glory. Amen.

Day: Eighth Today bring to Me - The Souls Who are detained in Purgatory,

and immerse them in the abyss of My mercy. Let the torrents of My Blood cool down their scorching flames. All these souls are greatly loved by Me. They are making retribution to My justice. It is in your power to bring them relief. Draw all the indulgences from the treasury of My Church and offer them on their behalf. Oh, if you only knew the torments they suffer, you would continually offer for them the alms of the spirit and pay off their debt to My justice.

Most merciful Jesus, You Yourself have said that You desire mercy; so I bring into the abode of Your most compassionate Heart the souls in Purgatory, souls who are very dear to You, and yet, must make retribution to Your justice. May the streams of blood and water which gushed forth from Your Heart put out the flames of Purgatory, that there, too, the power of Your mercy may be celebrated.

Eternal Father, turn Your merciful gaze upon the souls suffering in Purgatory, who are enfolded in the Most Compassionate Heart of Jesus. I beg You, by the sorrowful Passion of Jesus Your Son, and by all the bitterness with which His most sacred Soul was flooded: Manifest Your mercy to the souls who are under Your just scrutiny. Look upon them in no other way but only through the Wounds of Jesus, Your dearly beloved Son; for we firmly believe that there is no limit to Your goodness and compassion. Amen.

Ninth Day: Today bring to Me - Souls Who are Lukewarm,

and immerse them in the abyss of My mercy. These souls wound My Heart most painfully. My soul suffered the most dreadful loathing in the Garden of Olives because of lukewarm souls. They were the reason I cried out: "Father, take this cup away from Me, if it be Your will." For them the last hope of salvation is to turn to My mercy.

Most compassionate Jesus, You are compassion itself. I bring lukewarm souls into the abode of Your most compassionate Heart. In this fire of Your pure love let these tepid souls, who, like corpses, filled You with such deep loathing, be once again set aflame. O most compassionate Jesus, exercise the omnipotence of Your mercy and draw them into the very ardor of Your love, and bestow upon them the gift of holy love, for nothing is beyond Your power.

Eternal Father, turn Your merciful gaze upon lukewarm souls who are nonetheless enfolded in the most compassionate Heart of Jesus. Father of Mercy, I beg You by the bitter Passion of Your Son and by His three-hour agony on the Cross: Let them, too, glorify the abyss of Your mercy. Amen."*Diary of St. Faustina Kowalska: Divine Mercy in My Soul* © 1987 Marian Fathers of the Immaculate Conception, Stockbridge, MA 02163. Used with permission.

Appendix B

The Rosary Prayer:

The Rosary is a meditative prayer that takes us through the history of our redemption as written in the Bible, before each decade one asks grace for those one is interceding for.

The Apostles Creed: **see Appendix A**

Our Father: **see Appendix A**

Three Hail Mary's: **see Appendix A**
(On each decade of the mysteries one Our Father and ten Hail Marys)

<u>The Joyful Mysteries:</u>
1st Decade: The Annunciation of Jesus Christ's Birth. Luke 1:26-38.
2nd Decade: The Visitation of Mary to Elizabeth. Luke1:39-45, 56
3rd Decade: The Birth of Jesus Christ. Luke 2:1-21
4th Decade: The Presentation of Jesus to God in the Temple. Luke 2:22-38
5th Decade: The Finding of Jesus Christ in the Temple. Luke 2:41-52

The Luminious Mysteries:

1st Decade: The Baptism of Jesus Christ in River Jordan. Matt. 3:13-17

2nd Decade: The wedding at Cana. John 2:1-11

3rd Decade: The Proclamation of the Kingdom of God. Mark 2:2-12

4th Decade: The Transfiguration of Jesus Christ. Matt. 17:1-18

5th Decade: The Institution of the Eucharist. Luke 22:14-20

The Sorrowful Mysteries:

1st Decade: The Agony of Jesus Christ in the garden. Matt. 26:36-56

2nd Decade: Jesus Christ is Scourged at the pillar. Matt. 27:26

3rd Decade: Jesus Christ is Crowned with thorns. Matt. 27:27a;27-31

4th Decade: Jesus Christ carries the Cross. Matt. 27:32

5th Decade: Jesus Christ is crucified. Matt. 27:33-56

The Glorious Mysteries:

1st Decade: The Resurrection of Jesus Christ. John 20:1-29

2nd Decade: The Ascension of Jesus Christ into Heaven. Luke 24:36-53

3rd Decade: The Descent of the Holy Spirit. Acts 2:1-41

4th Decade: The Assumption of Blessed Virgin Mary. (As Enoch and Elijah went to Heaven; it is not a hard thing for God to do for Mary.)

5th Decade: The Crowning of Blessed Virgin Mary. Rev.12:1

Appendix C:

2 Maccabees 15:12-16 "What he saw was this: Onias, the former high priest, a good and virtuous man, modest in appearance, gentle in manners, distinguished in speech, trained from childhood in every virtuous practice, was praying with outstretched arms for the whole Jewish community. Then in the same way another man appeared, distinguished by his white hair and dignity, with an air about him of extraordinary majestic authority. Onias then said of him. "This is God's prophet Jeremiah, who loves his brethren and fervently prays for his people and their holy city." Stretching out his right hand, Jeremiah presented a gold sword to Judas. As he gave it to him he said, "Accept this holy sword as a gift from God; with it you shall crush your adversaries."

Appendix D:

2 Maccabees 12:43-46 "He then took up a collection among all soldiers, amounting to two thousand silver drachmas, which he sent to Jerusalem to provide for the expiatory sacrifice. In doing this he acted in very excellent and noble way, inasmuch as he had the resurrection of the dead in view; for if he were not expecting it, it would have been useless and foolish to pray for them in death. But if he did this with a view to the splendid reward that awaits those who had gone to rest in godliness, it was a holy and pious thought. Thus he made atonement for the dead that they might be freed from this sin."

Appendix E:

2 Maccabees 6:18 -7:41 "Eleazar, one of the foremost scribes, a man of advanced age and noble appearance, was being forced to open his mouth to eat pork. But preferring a glorious death to a life of defilement, he spat out the meat, and went forward to his own accord to the instrument of torture, as men ought to do who have the courage to reject the food which it is unlawful to taste even for the love of life.

Those in charge of that unlawful ritual meal took the man aside privately, because of their long acquaintance with him, and urged him to bring meat of his own providing, such as he could legitimately eat, and to pretend to be eating some of the meat of the sacrifice prescribed by the king; in this way he would escape the death penalty, and be treated kindly because of their old friendship with him. But he made up his mind in a noble manner, worthy of his years, the dignity of his advanced age, the merited distinction of his gray hair, and of the admirable life he had lived from childhood; and so he declared that above all he would be loyal to the holy laws given by God.

He told them to send him send him at once to the abode of the dead, explaining: "At our age it would be unbecoming to make such a pretense; many young men would think the ninety-year-old Eleazar had gone over to an alien religion. Should I thus dissimulate for the sake of a brief moment of life, they would be led astray by me, while I would bring shame and dishonor on my old age. Even if, for the time being, I avoid the punishment of men, I shall never, whether alive or dead, escape the hands of the Almighty. Therefore, by manfully giving up my life now, I will prove myself worthy of my old age, and I will leave to the young a noble example of how to die willing and generously for the revered and holy laws.'

He spoke thus, and went immediately to the instrument of torture. Those who shortly before had been kindly disposed, now became hostile toward him because what he had said seemed to them utter madness. When he was about to die under the blows, he groaned and said: "The LORD in his holy knowledge knows full well that, although I could have escaped death, I am not only enduring terrible pain in my body from scourging, but also suffering it with joy in my soul because of my devotion to him." This is how he died, leaving in his death a model of courage and an unforgettable example of virtue not only for the young but for the whole nation."

It also happened that seven brothers with their mother were arrested and tortured with whips and scourges by the king, to force them to eat pork in violation of God's law. One of the brothers, speaking for the others, said: "What do you expect to achieve by questioning us? We are ready to die rather than transgress the laws of our ancestors." At that the king, in fury, gave orders to have pans and caldrons heated. While they were being heated, he commanded his executioners to cut out the tongue of the one who had spoken for the others, to scalp him and cut off his hands and feet, while the rest of his brothers and his mother looked on. When he was completely maimed but still breathing, the king ordered them to carry him to the fire and fry him. As a cloud of smoke spread from the pan, the brothers and their mother encouraged one another to die bravely, saying such words as these: "The LORD GOD is looking on, and He truly has compassion on us, as Moses declared in his canticle, when he protested openly with the words, 'And he will have pity on his servants.'"

When the first brother had died in this manner they brought the second to be made sport of. After tearing off the skin and hair of his head, they asked him, "Will you eat pork rather than have your body tortured limb by limb?" Answering in the language of his forefathers, he said, "Never!" So he too in turn suffered the same tortures as the first. At the point of death he said: "You accursed fiend, you are depriving us of this present life, but the King of the world will raise us up to live again forever. It is for his laws that we are dying."

After him the third suffered their cruel sport. He put out his tongue at once when told to do so, and bravely held out his hands, as he spoke these noble words: "It was from Heaven that I received these; for the sake of his laws I disdain them; from him I hope to receive them again." Even the king and his attendants marveled at the young man's courage, because he regarded his sufferings as nothing.

After he had died, they tortured and maltreated the fourth brother in the same way. When he was near death, he said, "It is my choice to die at the hands of men with the God-given hope of being restored to life by him; but for you, there will be no resurrection to life."

They next brought forward the fifth brother and maltreated him. Looking at the king, he said; "Since you have power among men, mortal though you are, do what you please. But do not think that our nation is forsaken by God. Only wait and you will see how his great power will torment you and your descendants." After him they brought the sixth brother. When he was about to die, he said: "Have no vain illusions. We suffer these things on our account, because we have sinned against our God; that is why such astonishing things have happened to us. Do not think, then, that you will go unpunished for having dared to fight against God."

Most admirable and worthy of everlasting remembrance was the mother, who saw her seven sons perish in a single day, yet bore it courageously because her hope in the LORD. Filled with a noble spirit that stirred her manly courage, she exhorted each of them in the language of their forefather with these words: "I do not know how you came into existence in my womb; it was not I who gave you the breath of life, nor was it I who set in order the elements of which of you is composed. Therefore, since it is the Creator of the universe who shapes each man's beginning, as he brings about the origin of everything, he, in his mercy, will give you back both breath and life, because you now disregard yourselves for the sake of his law.

Antiochus, suspecting insult in her words, thought he was being ridiculed. As the youngest brother was still alive, the king appealed to him, not with mere words, but with promises on oath, to make him rich and happy if he would abandon his ancestral customs: he would make him his Friend and entrust him with high office. When the youth paid no attention to him at all, the king appealed to the mother, urging her to advise her boy to save his life. After he had urged her for a long time, she went through the motions of persuading her son. In derision of the cruel tyrant, she leaned over close to her son and said in their native language: "Son, have pity on me, who carried you in my womb for nine months, nursed you for three years, brought you up, educated and supported you to your present age. I beg you, child, to look at the heavens and the earth and see all that is in them; then you will know that God did not make them out of existing things; and in the same way the human race came into existence. Do not be afraid of this executioner, but be worthy of your brothers and accept death, so that in the time of mercy I may receive you again with them."

She had scarcely finished speaking when the youth said: "What are you waiting for? I will not obey the king's command. I obey the command of the law given to our forefathers through Moses. But you have contrived every kind of affliction for the Hebrews, will not escape the hands of God. We, indeed, are suffering because of our sins. Though our living LORD treats us harshly for a little to correct us with chastisements, he will again be reconciled with his servants. But you, wretch, vilest of all men! Do not, in your insolence, concern yourself with unfounded hopes, as you raise your hand against the children of Heaven. You have not yet escaped the judgment of the Almighty and all seeing God.

My brothers, after enduring brief pain, have drunk of never-failing life, under God's covenant, but you, by the judgment of God, shall receive just punishments for your arrogance. Like my brothers, I offer up my body and my life for our ancestral laws, imploring God to show mercy soon to our nation, and by afflictions and blows to make you confess that he alone is God. Through me and my brothers, may there be an end to the wrath of the Almighty that has fallen on our whole nation." At that, the king became enraged and treated him even worse than the others, since he bitterly resented the boy's contempt. Thus he too died undefiled, putting all his trust in the LORD. The mother was last to die, after her sons.

34. Bibliography

1. "Confessions of a Mega Church Pastor." How I discovered the Hidden Treasure in the Catholic Church. By Allen Hunt, Beacon Publishing, 15 February, 2010 ph. 978-750-8400; fax 978-646-8600.
2. "The Divine Mercy Message and Devotion. From Diary of St. Faustina". By Fr. Seraphim Micalenko, MIC with Vinny Flynn and Robert A. Stackpole, Marian Press, 2006, Stockbridge, MA 02163. 1-800-462-7426
3. "God Calling By Two Listeners" Edited by A.J. Russell 28th Edition April 1970
4. "The Incorruptibles." By Joan C. Cruz, Tan Books, 1977 P.O. Box 410487, Charlotte, N.C. 28241
5. "Our Lady of Fatima Peace Plan from Heaven." Tan Books and Publishers, 1983 P.O. Box 410487, Charlotte, N.C. 28241
6. "The Miracles of the Eucharist." By Joan C. Cruz, Tan Books, 1977 P.O. Box 410487, Charlotte, N.C. 28241
7. "The New American Bible" 1991 World Catholic Press a division of Catholic Book Publishing Corp. © USCCB, CCD, 3211 Fourth Street, N.E. Washington, D.C. 20017-1194
8. "The Secret of the Rosary." By St. Louis de Montfort, Tan books, July 2005 P.O. Box 410487, Charlotte, N.C. 28241
9. "Shalom and Israel. A message of peace in Israel's postage stamps." Chapter Two Books, Fountain House, 3 Conduit Mews, London, SE 18 7AP, United Kingdom; Gift of God Nathanael literature distributors, 64 Hills Road, Ajax, Ontario, L1S 2W4 Canada
10. "Scriptural Basis for Marian Doctrine and Devotion Questions and Answers." By Rev. John H. Hampsch, C.M.F. Queenship Publishing Company 805-957-4893* 800-647-9882 ph; 805-957-1631

11. "Through the Year with Fulton Sheen Inspirational Readings for each day of the year." Compiled and edited by Henry Dieterich. Ignatius Press San Francisco 2003
12. www.BiblicalCatholic.com David Armstrong
13. www.CatholicBridge.com David MacDonald
14. www.newadvent.org Kevin Knight
15. Siddur Tehilla HASHEM, Nusach Ha-Ari Zal 5748 - 1988. MerkosL'InyoneiChinuch, Inc. Brooklyn, New York 11213

35. **Further reading and research:**
    A. www.chnetworking.org for The Journey Home testimonies of Clergy and laity from Anglican, Baptists, Lutherans, Presbyterians etc. who were led back to the Catholic Church.
    B. The www.ewtn.org
    C. *"The Apostolate of Holy Motherhood."* Complied by Mark I. Miravalle, S.T.D. P.O. Box 227, Geneva, OH 44041 A great book for all mothers; and fathers too. A great book to check out about the dying the graces for heathens and pagans p.61 first paragraph. I could not quote due to the policy of copyright owners.
    D. www.CatholicAnswers.org
    E. *Imitations of Christ* by Thomas a Kempis
    F. *Imitations of Mary* by Thomas a Kempis
    G. *Documents of Fatima & Memoirs of Sr. Lucia* by Fr. Antonio M. Martins, S.J.
    H. *Our Lady of Guadalupe* by Carl Anderson & Msgr. Eduardo Chavez
    I. *Our Lady of Kibeho* Mary speaks to the world from the heart of Africa by Immaculee Ilibagiza with Steve Erwin Hay House, P.O. Box 5100, Carlsbad, CA 92018-5100 1-800-654-5126
    J. *Our Lady of Lourdes* by Bob & Penny Lord
    K. *Padre Pio the Wonder Worker* an anthology compiled by Bro. Francis Mary Kalvelage
    F.I.

36. Israel's Place in the Bible: I am writing this because of some Christians' perspective on the people and the land.

The People

Due to writings and comments of Catholic and non-Catholic brethren on Israel, that the Church has replaced Israel. I felt I should do a write up on what I have read in the Scriptures about Israel's place in God's covenant plan; it has not changed. It still stands. Several passages in the Scriptures confirm this. With people's writings and God waiting for the number of the Gentiles to be fulfilled makes it seem as if the Church has replaced Israel. This is Israel as a nation not as a religion will come to believe in Jesus Christ and us Christians and they form the One New Person (Catholic Bible)/One New Man (NKJV). Ephesians 2:15 "Abolishing the law with its commandments and legal claims, that He might create in Himself one new person in place of two, thus establishing peace."

In Romans 11:17-18 it says, *"But if some of the branches were broken off, and you, a wild olive shoot, were grafted in their place and have come to share in the rich root of the olive tree, do not boast against the branches. If you do boast, consider that you do not support the root; the root supports you."*

Again in Roman's 11:25-29 it furthers the thought, *"I do not want you to be unaware of this mystery, brothers, so that you will not become wise [in] your own estimation: a hardening has come upon Israel in part, until the full number of the Gentiles comes in, and thus all Israel will be saved, as it is written: 'The deliverer will come out of Zion, He will turn away godlessness from Jacob; and this is My covenant with them when I take away their sins.' In respect to the gospel, they are enemies on your account; but in respect to election, they are beloved because of the patriarchs. For the gifts and call of God are irrevocable."*

In 2 Corinthians 3:14-16 it makes the thought clearer, *"Rather, their thoughts were rendered dull, for to this present day the same veil remains unlifted when they read the old covenant, because through Christ it is taken away. To this day, in fact, whenever Moses is read, a veil lies over their hearts, but when a person turns to the Lord the veil is removed."*

Equally important, is Paul's Epistle to the Ephesians 2:11-20 he exhorts them thus, *"Therefore, remember that at one time you, Gentiles in the flesh, called the uncircumcision by those called the circumcision, which is done in the flesh by human hands, were at that time without Christ, alienated from the community of Israel and strangers to the covenants of promise, without hope and without God in the world. But now in Christ Jesus you who once were far off have become near by the Blood of Christ. For He is our peace, He who made both one and broke down the dividing wall of enmity, through His flesh, abolishing the law with its commandments and legal claims, that He might create in Himself one new person (one new man) in place of the two, thus establishing peace, and might reconcile both with God, in one body, through the cross, putting that enmity to death by it. He preached peace to you who were far off and peace to those who were near, for through Him we both have access in one Spirit to the Father. So then you are no longer strangers and sojourners, but you are fellow citizens with the holy ones and members of the household of God, built upon the foundations of the apostles and prophets, with Christ Jesus Himself as the capstone."* Paul now affirms thus in Ephesians 3:6, *"That the Gentiles are coheirs, members of the same body, and copartners in the promise in Jesus Christ through the gospel."*

In the parable of the tenants (Mark 12: 1-12): where the tenants killed the son, the owner now gave the vineyards to others. Seems like gentile Christians replaced the Israelites; rather the leadership of the Lord's vineyard is taken from the priestly lineage [hereditary] to the ordinary people: thus, the apostles now were given the leadership of the Lord's vineyard but still maintained the principles of the priestly office.

In the Bible I have not yet come across any Scripture that says the Gentile Christians have replaced Israel. By two immutable things it is impossible for God to lie, thus by the above Scriptures it is impossible for God to lie. In Isaiah 40:8 it says, *"Though the grass withers and the flower wilts, the word of our God stands forever."* Jesus said none of God's word will be left unfulfilled.

Biblical Perspective on the Land of Israel

In Jeremiah 16:14-15, it says: *"However, days will surely come, says the Lord, when it will no longer be said, As the Lord lives, who brought the*

Israelites out of Egypt;" but rather, "As the Lord lives, who brought the Israelites out of the lands of the north and out of all the countries to which he had banished them." "I will bring them back to the land which I gave their fathers."

Again, in Jeremiah 23:7-8 it reiterates the above Scripture with a slight variation, *"Therefore, the days will come, says the Lord, when they shall no longer, say, "As the Lord lives, who brought the Israelites out of the land of Egypt;" but rather, "As the Lord lives, who brought the descendants of the house of Israel up from the land of the north" –and from all the lands to which I banished them; they shall again live on their own land."*

Furthermore, in Ezekiel 17:11 *"I will gather you from the nations and assemble you from the countries over which you have been scattered, and I will restore to you the land of Israel."* It is repeated in Ezekiel 20:33-34 *"As I live, says the Lord God, with a mighty hand and outstretched arm, with poured-out wrath, I swear I will be king over you! With a mighty hand and outstretched arm, with poured-out wrath, I will bring you out from the nations and gather you from the countries over which you are scattered."*

In Isaiah 61:9 it says, *"Their descendants shall be renowned among the nations, and their offspring among the peoples; all who see them shall acknowledge them as a race the Lord has blessed."*

To confirm the above Scripture here is an observation from a publication, "With less than 1% of the world's population, Israel has produced 10% of the Nobel prize winners." *Shalom and Israel: a message of peace in Israel's postage stamps©* Nathanael literature distributors and Chapter Two Books, Fountain House, 3 Conduit Mews, London, SE 18 7AP, United Kingdom. Used with permission.

In Zechariah 1:17 it speaks of the prosperities of her cities, *"Proclaim further: Thus says the Lord of hosts: My cities shall again overflow with prosperity; the Lord will again comfort Zion, and again choose Jerusalem."*

Jeremy Ben Ami [a Jewish political activist] in his book *New Voice for Israel* sums up Isaiah and Zechariah 1:17 succulently, "Economically, Israel's success is mind-boggling. The small nation has more start-up companies than any other country in the world (one for every 1,844 Israelis as of 2009), and more listings on the NASDAQ stock exchange than any country other than the United States (63, as of 2008). Israel leads the world in the percentage of its economy spent on research and development. In 2008, per capita venture capital investments in Israel were 2.5 times greater than in the United States, more than 30 times than in Europe, 80 times greater than in China and 350 times greater than in India."

God is a covenant keeping God. He made several covenants in the Bible with the Patriarchs. In Jeremiah 31:31-38; 40c it says, "*The days are coming, says the Lord, when I will make a new covenant with the house of Israel and the house of Judah. It will not be like the covenant I made with their fathers the day I took them by the hand to lead them forth from the land of Egypt; for they broke my covenant and I had to show Myself their Master, says the Lord. But this is the covenant which I will make with the house of Israel after those days, says the Lord. I will place My law within them, and write it upon their hearts; I will be their God, and they shall be My people. No longer will they have need to teach their friends and kinsmen how to know the Lord. All, from least to greatest, shall know Me, says the Lord, for I will forgive their evil doing and remember their sin no more." Thus says the Lord, He Who gives the sun to light the day, moon and stars to light the night; Who stirs the sea up till its waves roar, whose name is Lord of Hosts: If ever these natural laws give way in spite of Me, says the Lord, then shall the race of Israel cease as a nation before Me forever. Thus says the Lord: If the heavens on high can be measured, or the foundations below the earth be sounded, then will I cast off the whole race of Israel because of all they have done, says the Lord." "The days are coming, says the Lord, when the city shall be rebuilt as the Lord's, from the Tower of Hananel to the Corner Gate." "Never again shall the city be rooted up or thrown down."*

"For the peace of Jerusalem pray: 'May those who love you prosper! May peace be within your ramparts, prosperity within your towers.'" Psalm 122:6

Isaiah 62:1 *"For Zion's sake I will not be silent, for Jerusalem's sake I will not be quiet, until her vindication shines forth like dawn and her victory like a burning torch."*

Jesus' word, *"Behold, your house will be abandoned, desolate. I tell you, you will not see Me again until you say, 'Blessed is He who comes in the name of the Lord.'"* Matthew 23:38-39

Another Scripture that points out that the people of Israel still matters to God and has not been displaced by the gentile Christians is Romans 9:29 where Paul quotes Isaiah 1:9, *"And as Isaiah predicted: 'Unless the Lord of Hosts had left us descendants, we would have become like Sodom and have been made like Gomorrah.'"* Consequently, God's plan for land of Israel and her people to exist and be in the land He gave them through His covenant with Abraham, Isaac and Jacob still stands and will be fulfilled at the appointed time. If not He would not have made it possible for them to get the land in the first place. It would have failed.

Furthermore, *"He made from one the whole human race to dwell on the entire surface of the earth, and He fixed the ordered seasons and the boundaries of their regions."* Acts 17:26

Consequently, God has worked it out so that the nation was restored in 1948; if God did not want it reestablished (to fulfill His Word), He would not have revealed the above Scriptures in preparation for what He intends to do at this time in world history. Furthermore, the miracle of the 1967 and 1973 Wars speaks for itself. See below for a testimony on the 1973 War.

This is certainly a divine intervention, to confirm that God has not changed His mind concerning the people of Israel and the land of Israel; can be seen in the excerpt from

"Miracles Can Be Yours Today" by Pat Robertson a narration of what God did for Israel when they were attacked unawares in 1973; **"Stories have come out of the modern nation of Israel about battlefield miracles brought on by angels, like this remarkable account told me personally by Effie, a former Israeli Army Brigadier General who has become an orthodox rabbi."**

"On Yom Kippur in 1973, the holiest day in the Jewish calendar, when almost all Jews were fasting and praying to seek atonement from God, the combined armies of Egypt, Syria, and Jordan launched an unprovoked attack on Israel. Israel's military reserves were hastily called from their prayers into their airplanes, battle tanks, half-tracks, and infantry units to repel hostile troops gathered at their borders. That flat plateau that becomes the Golan Heights extends from Damascus for about fifty miles before it drops off sharply to the rich agricultural Hula and Jordan valleys on the west, and to the Sea of Galilee and the city of Tiberius on the south.

"The Syrians held high ground. Before their attack, they had amassed one thousand or more battle tanks on this high plateau, from which they could direct punishing artillery or mortar fire at the unprotected Jewish settlers living below.

"The Israeli Defense Force had to rush to battle positions and then claw their way up the steep heights to confront the oncoming Syrians. Military historians have said that this was the fiercest tank battle since World War II in Europe.

"Effie Eitam was a company commander who was ordered forward into bitter battle, merciless struggle where men were dropping all around him. Then he received a nerve-chilling order: "infiltrate the Syrians lines, make your way to the command post of the commanding general of the lead tank division, and kill or capture him."

"This was a mission fraught with peril. The chances of success were almost nonexistent. But the peril to the nation was so great that boldness and daring were demanded. There was no time for restraint and caution. As Eitam led his company forward into the haze of battle smoke, he saw a bright being standing in the smoke. He thought it was a Syrian soldier guarding the division command post, so he raised his rifle to fire. Then to his amazement, the figure turned into a dove that flew out of the smoke of the battle straight at him.

"The bird rested on the shoulder he needed to fire his weapon, so he brushed it away. It then fluttered over to his other shoulder, where it remained for the next ten days, occasionally fluttering to his outstretched hand, then back to his shoulder. The bird never left him during some of the most vicious tank, artillery, and hand-to-hand infantry fighting in the history of warfare.

"Day after day, Eitam checked his unit for casualties. Day after day, not one man was killed or wounded. Day after day after day, while death and carnage were all around them, his unit suffered no casualties. Day after day, the dove stayed perched on his shoulder.

"Finally, the Israeli forces drove deep across the Golan into Syria territory. Eitam's unit had done its job, and it was reassigned to rear, the dove flew away and was never seen again." *"Miracles Can Be Yours Today"* © CBN Publication, 977 Centerville Turnpike, Virginia Beach, VA 23464 Used with permission.

Another modern day version of David versus Goliath was that of Brigadier-General Avigdor Kahalani in the 1973 War, as he faced the massive Syrian armada with just seven (7) tanks. When you get the chance watch *The 77th Battalion Documentary Film,* based on the book *OZ 77.* Brigadier-General Kahalani was the Commander of the armored division in the war.

Of note worthy is Ben Gurion, Israeli Premier's testimony an excerpt from the booklet *"Shalom and Israel: a message in Israel's postage stamps."* He was asked what part of the Bible had had in the rebirth of Israel. 'Everything,' was the Prime Minister's answer. 'Without the Bible we would not have been able to do anything. The Bible told us that we should rebuild and recreate this land; we are doing this with might and main, and we shall succeed. The Bible says that we should cultivate the land; we are already doing that, and we are getting extensive woods and meadows and farming areas. After 30 Centuries the Books of the Bible are still the source of our knowledge!" *"Shalom and Israel: a message in Israel's postage stamps."* © Nathanael literature distributors and Chapter Two Books, Fountain House, 3 Conduit Mews, London, S.E. 18 7 AP United Kingdom. Used with permission.

Bibliography II

1. "God Calling By Two Listeners" Edited by A.J. Russell 28th Edition April 1970
2. "Miracles Can Be Yours Today." By Pat Robertson, CBN Publication, 977 Centerville Turnpike, Virginia Beach, VA 23464
3. "New Voice for Israel." By Jeremy Ben Ami
4. "Shalom and Israel, A message of peace in Israel's postage stamps." Gift of God Nathanael literature distributors, and Chapter Two Books, Fountain House, 3 Conduit Mews, London, SE 18 7 AP, United Kingdom

Postscript
2014 - 2015
Since the last publication of this book in December 2013, the Holy Spirit has prompted me with new materials to substantiate the dire need to reconcile. The writings I came across convinced me of the need for the wounds of Jesus Christ to heal, which the unity of Christians will do. Jesus Christ's wounds have not healed. They are mystical wounds as stated in the Divine Mercy Novena Day 5 see * asterisks below.

To start with a non-Catholic writing – *Heaven is for Real*, by Todd Burpo with Lynn Vincent. Colton Burpo told his dad Todd Burpo that Jesus Christ has red markers on His Hands *and* Feet check page 69 in *Heaven is for Real* © Thomas Nelson Publishers, Nashville, TN. I deduced that he could only see Jesus' Hand and Feet, and not His Heart because of Jesus' clothing. Also, healed wounds are not red except for fresh wounds. Remember this as we move to the next writing from a Catholic source.

As we have prophets in non-Catholic Churches so do we have in Catholic Churches. Each one of us has been given spiritual gifts. A message and a prayer from Barnabas Nwoye and his spiritual director, Fr. Evaristus Eshiowu, FSSP [The Priestly Fraternity of St. Peter] – "This is the Devotion to the Precious Blood of Our Lord Jesus Christ as given by Our Lord and Our Lady and a multitude of angels and saints to a nearly illiterate teenage boy, Barnabas Nwoye, in the village of Olo, Enugu State, Nigeria from 1985 to 2003. Our Lord told the young boy, Barnabas, that this is the greatest devotion He has given to the Church and the last one He will give in this age. This is the ark that will protect and bring the Holy Catholic Church, the remnant faithful and all those you love and pray for safety through bitter trials of the coming chastisement and into the promised Era of Peace." The prayer on *The Holy Chaplet of the MOSTPRECIOUS BLOOD OF OUR LORD JESUS CHRIST* – a prayer point reads:
"Leader: O Most Precious Blood of Jesus Christ."
"Response: Heal the wounds in the Most Sacred Heart of Jesus."
http://www.preciousbloodinternational.com/prayers_02.html
http://www.preciousbloodinternational.com

© Association of the Precious Blood, P.O. Box 15851, Tallahassee, FL 32317 used with permission.

In section 17 of this book, I discussed the Divine Mercy Novena from St. Faustina circa 1935. *The Divine Mercy Novena Day 5 reads: "Today bring to Me SOULS OF THOSE WHO HAVE SEPARATED THEMSELVES FROM MY CHURCH, and immerse them in the ocean of My mercy. During My bitter Passion they tore at My Body and Heart, that is, My Church. As they return to unity with the Church My wounds heal in this way they alleviate My Passion." © Divine Mercy Message and Devotion Revised Edition, Marian Press, Stockbridge, MA 01263 used with permission.

The Divine Mercy Novena Day 5 truly wraps it up and consolidates the two writings above as regards the dire need to reconcile and embrace one another. Consider Jesus Christ's agony at the Garden of Gethsemane, and on the Cross before He breathed His last. He offered Himself freely for the salvation of the Body of Christ and for all mankind. Let us unite in the Body of Christ to help heal His wounds!

2013
After the publication of the e-book version of this book several things has happened which needs to be brought to light one of them which in the words of Fr. Charles Cummings, O.C.S.O, this is God's stamp of approval to the e-book.

I will report on two people: First, on Pope Francis: On Wednesday, June 19, 2013 called for Christian unity among Christians and said it was the gift of the Holy Spirit. He made an "off cuff remark" "he spent roughly 40 minutes praying with an evangelical pastor before leaving his residence today where both prayed to seek unity among Christians. And Jesus Christ sends us the Holy Spirit to build unity." After this remark on the balcony, he went down to St. Peter's Square to meet and mingle with the people a white dove perched on his fingers! See the article and picture at the end of the book. His call for unity and the white dove in a nut shell tied in with the contents and cover of my e-book published on May 12, 2013 which is in hard copy. http://www.zenit.org/

The other is a post by Charles Shamp on Elijahlist a non-denominational Christian website, on Wednesday, July 17, 2013, I will quote the last few paragraphs, for the whole post see end of the book. "While we have come far in the breakdown of racial barriers, one of A.A. Allen's prayers in my dream was that we become even more united in the Church, that God would indeed breakdown the wall of segregation in our hearts. While I know in part he was addressing the issue of race, I believe he meant more than just the color of our skin. I believe he was praying for unity across denominational lines as well, that the Church would be united as a whole with one sole purpose, and Jesus Christ would be glorified in the earth. I believe in God emphasizing this point of unity right now to take us beyond where we have been. In the coming days look for more churches to be crossing denominational lines and cross pollinating as God shatters the walls of separation that have held us in for too long, ineffective for His Kingdom."
http://www.elijahlist.com/

Pope Francis Calls For Unity Among Christians
Recounting the event of the conversion of St. Paul, the Pope said that the words of Christ, "I am Jesus whom you are persecuting", indicate the deep union that exists between Christians and Christ." "When Jesus ascended into heaven he did not leave us orphans, but with the gift of the Holy Spirit, our union with Him has become even more intense," the Pope said. "The Second Vatican Council says that Jesus" communicating His Spirit, Christ made His brothers, called together from all nations, mystically the components of His own Body."

The image of the body in St. Paul's Letter to the Corinthians helps us to understand the depth of what the Holy Father described as the "Church-Christ bond." The Church, the Pope said, "is not a charitable, cultural or political association, but a living body, that walks and acts in history."

"And this body has a head, Jesus, who guides, feeds and supports it. This is a point I want to emphasize: if the head is separated from the rest of the body, the whole person cannot survive. So it is in the Church, we must remain bound ever more deeply to Jesus. But not only that: just as the body needs the lifeblood to keep it alive, so we must allow Jesus to work in us, that His Word guide us, that His presence in the Eucharist nourish us, animate us, that His love gives strength to our love of neighbor. And this always!

Though Many, We Are One

Reflecting on the second aspect of the Church as the Body of Christ, Pope Francis told the pilgrims that although the Church consists of a diverse variety of people, "we form one body, as we were all baptized by one Spirit into one body."

The communion and unity that exists between Christians, he continued, show the richness of the gifts distributed by the Holy Spirit.

"Let us remember this well," the Pope exhorted the faithful, "being part of the Church means being united to Christ and receiving from Him the divine life that makes us live as Christians; it means remaining united to the Pope and the Bishops who are instruments of unity and communion, and also means overcoming personal interests and divisions, in order to understand each other better, to harmonize the variety and richness of each member; in a word, to love God and the people who are next to us more, in the family, in the parish, in the associations."

Pope Francis also emphasized the need for unity among all Christian communities, saying that in order for the Body to live, all its limbs must be united. Unity, he exclaimed, "is beyond all conflict."

The Holy Father also decried the damage that is done by internal struggles, selfishness and gossip.

"Never gossip about others, never!," the Pope exclaimed. "How much damage divisions among Christians, being partisan, narrow interests causes to the Church,! Divisions among us, but also divisions among the communities: evangelical Christians, orthodox Christians, Catholic Christians, but why divided? We must try to bring about unity."

Continuing his off the cuff remarks, the Holy Father told the crowds that he spent roughly 40 minutes praying with an evangelical pastor before leaving his residence today where both prayed to seek unity among Christians.

"We Catholics must pray with each other and other Christians," the Holy Father concluded. "Pray that the Lord gift us unity! Unity among ourselves! How will we ever have unity among Christians if we are not capable of having it among us Catholics,...in the family, how many families fight and split up? Seek unity, unity builds the Church and comes from Jesus Christ. He sends us the Holy Spirit to build unity!"

http://www.zenit.org/en/articles/37469

Picture of Pope Francis at St. Peter's Square grounds, after his Wednesday, June 19, 2013 General Audience… where he called for unity among Christians, and he said it is the gift of the Holy Spirit.

Charles Shamp: Our Prophetic Declarations and Dreams are Becoming Reality in this Season

Charles and Brynn Shamp, Avenue of Dreams

God has always delighted greatly in communicating with His children throughout history. Typically, our main source of communication comes through prayer and reading the Word, yet God can and will use other ways to speak to and direct people. Another source in which God speaks is through the **avenue of dreams**. Yes, that's right, even in sleep our spirit can encounter the supernatural and receive direction from the throne of God.

Throughout the chapters of the Bible, we see many accounts where people were visited by God through dreams. In both the Old and New Testaments, dreams are mentioned over a hundred times as a source and means by which God speaks to men. In fact, the Book of Acts clearly states that in the last days there will be an outpouring of dreams - so it is evident that **God has more to say to us concerning our destinies in this day and age, and He wants to use dreams to articulate His message to us.**

For God speaketh once, yea twice, yet man perceiveth it not. In a dream, in a vision of the night, when deep sleep falleth upon men, in slumberings upon the bed; then He openeth the ears of men, and sealeth their instruction... Job 33:14-16

Webster's dictionary defines a dream as a series of thoughts, images, or emotions that appear in our mind during sleep. There are four main purposes that I have seen through Scripture in which God uses dreams to communicate:

1. To reveal revelation to those standing in a prophetic office (see Numbers 12:6).
2. To reveal divine purpose and destiny for our lives (see Genesis 37:5-8).
3. To counsel and advise leaders, kings, and presidents of certain coming world circumstances (see Genesis 41:1-8).
4. To release impartation to step into a greater dimension of power and authority (see 1 Kings 3:5-15).

Personally, I am not one who dreams very often, but on the rare occasion that I do, God seems to send me a message either for my personal life or for the corporate Body of Christ. Recently, while spending some time with my family in the mountains, God visited me in a dream that I know will bear witness with many. It carries great significance for where we are heading in the coming days as **God is awakening this generation to a fresh outpouring of the Spirit.**

Healing Revivalists

On Friday, June 28, early in the morning hours, I was taken into a dream. In this dream I found myself in an old church lobby that I recognized from my childhood. It was an Assembly of God church where, as a youth, I had first experienced the baptism of the Holy Spirit and spoke in tongues. As I stood there remembering what God had done for me so many years ago, in walked two sharply dressed preachers in black suits. **I immediately recognized them as prominent healing revivalists from the past that God had used mightily in America.**

Looking around as though they were searching for someone or something, they turned to see me standing there. With eager excitement on both of their faces, they approached me to engage in what I believed was going to be a conversation. To my utter astonishment, standing before me was the late great **R. W. Schambach**, and his predecessor, the man of faith and power, **A. A. Allen**. Without a word spoken between us, they embraced me in a hug and immediately began to pray with great fervency.

Their prayer was that of sanctification, consecration, and impartation, not for me alone but for the Church and this generation of preachers; a prayer that our faith would not fail in these difficult times; and that God would once again grant to us a sweeping revival across this great nation.

As they prayed, such surges of power swept through my body that I began to cry and shake violently. I felt as though I could take no more. So much revelation was being conveyed during these moments, and yet I was still able to hear every word as it released power and impartation into my spirit man.

Even as I write this, I can hear their voices resound inside me, as though they were praying once again. Every point of the prayer was articulated with Holy Spirit precision, perfection, and power. Suddenly, I was awakened in my bed with the tangible power and presence of the Holy Spirit all over my body.

While there is much symbolism that I could touch on, after much prayer, I have concluded that the Lord would have me share **four significant points of interest** within the prayer and dream that have prophetic instruction and edification for us as we come into what I believe is **a season of fresh visitation for us both individually and corporately.**

A Voice of Healing Returns

During the prayer, both Brother Allen and Brother Schambach prayed that **God would release great faith and boldness for miracles to this generation**. They prayed that we would stand on their shoulders and push into greater realms of supernatural power and see things they never saw during their lifetimes.

One of the greatest points that I believe God was trying to get across through this dream is that we are on the verge of a fresh move of the Spirit across this country.

In this hour, God is releasing mantles of faith from previous generations to all those who will receive them.

Beloved, when I gave all diligence to write unto you of the common salvation, it was needful for me to write unto you, and exhort you that ye should earnestly contend for the faith which was once delivered unto the saints. Jude 3

One thing is very clear: These two men represent not only the faith of a past generation, but also one of the greatest times of revival to ever take place in this nation. A revival that not only touched one special location within our country, but spread across this great land to many of our wonderful towns and cities. There is a reemergence of what I call the revival road. **Along this road are cities where God will move in the coming days with great campaigns of revival and healing as He did in the past.**

Strengthen ye the weak hands, and confirm the feeble knees. Say to them that are of a fearful heart, "Be strong, fear not: behold, your God will come with vengeance, even God with a recompense; he will come and save you."

Then the eyes of the blind shall be opened, and the ears of the deaf shall be unstopped. Then shall the lame man leap as an hart, and the tongue of the dumb sing: for in the wilderness shall waters break out, and streams in the desert. And the parched ground shall become a pool, and the thirsty land springs of water: in the habitation of dragons, where each lay, shall be grass with reeds and rushes.

And an highway shall be there, and a way, and it shall be called "The way of holiness"; the unclean shall not pass over it; but it shall be for those: the wayfaring men, though fools, shall not err therein. Isaiah 35:3-8

Seven Cities

Here is a list of seven cities that were deposited within my spirit as cities of revival and healing during the dream:

1. Detroit, Michigan
2. Dallas, Texas
3. St. Louis, Missouri
4. Birmingham, Alabama
5. Chicago, Illinois
6. Oklahoma City, Oklahoma
7. Philadelphia, Pennsylvania

The Miracle Is In the Valley

During the life of A. A. Allen, God blessed him with a wonderful ministry center in Arizona, which he named Miracle Valley. Over the years this place has seen great devastation, but I believe God is going to restore that land to its former glory and it will stand as a memorial and monument of what He did in our nation.

Likewise, some that are reading this have experienced devastation over the past few years in their personal life, both spiritually and physically. A place of barrenness. A time of living in the valley. This is what many have been feeling. As if their spiritual warfare will not end. While in the dream, God conveyed this message of hope and strength to those who are weary in well doing: **There is a miracle in your valley!**

The voice of him that crieth in the wilderness, "Prepare ye the way of the Lord, make straight in the desert a highway for our God. Every valley shall be exalted, and every mountain and hill shall be made low: and the crooked shall be made straight, and the rough places plain: And the glory of the Lord shall be revealed, and all flesh shall see it together: for the mouth of the Lord hath spoken it." Isaiah 40:3-5

Some have felt like they have dug themselves into a hole of despair that they can't get out of. Depression has come in and left some hopeless in this season. **I want to tell you that what seems to be a valley of dry bones and death will, in this next six months, become a valley of miracles.** The miracles that are coming your way will catch your enemies by surprise! Get ready for God to fill your ditch!

And he said, "Thus saith the Lord, 'Make this valley full of ditches.' For thus saith the Lord, 'Ye shall not see wind, neither shall ye see rain; yet that valley shall be filled with water, that ye may drink, both ye, and your cattle, and your beasts. And this is but a light thing in the sight of the Lord: He will deliver the Moabites also into your hand.'" 2 Kings 3:16-18

The Hearts of the Fathers Turn To the Sons

It is well known that during Brother Schambach's life he was mentored and imparted to by Brother Allen. As a young man, R. W. worked so closely with Allen that many believe that he received Allan's miracle mantle after he went to be with the Lord in 1970, much like Elijah passed his mantle to his younger apprentice Elisha right before he was caught away into Heaven. R. W. received something special from A. A. Allen.

As previously mentioned, I believe there is once again a passing of the mantle to this generation, but I also believe something else is taking place in this hour. In the dream, R. W. appeared to be a young man who was working with Brother Allen. There was a love and friendship you could feel that they had for one another as they prayed and prophesied in the dream. You could feel that they truly honored each other even though you could see that A. A. Allen was older and seemed to be training R. W. for the ministry. The Bible says in Malachi:

"Behold, I will send you Elijah the prophet before the coming of the great and dreadful day of the Lord: And he shall turn the heart of the fathers to the children, and the heart of the children to their fathers, lest I come and smite the earth with a curse" (Malachi 4:5-6).

The anointing of Elijah is one that connects fathers and sons in the unity of the faith. **There is a real blessing coming to ministries and spiritual fathers who will honor and work with their sons in this season**. The Bible says that one can put a thousand to flight, but two can put ten thousand. You will see in the coming days more revivals that have older, seasoned ministers working with younger evangelists. **The harvest that is coming is mighty, and we need the passion of the young mixed with experience of the mature to bring it in**. Heaven is certainly counting on our generation to see this come to pass!

Unity In the Assembly of the Saints

One of A. A. Allen's greatest accomplishments in ministry was breaking down racial barriers and segregation by allowing all races and colors to worship God under the same tent. In fact, he was one of the first Caucasian ministers to have an all African-American choir during his tent revivals. In an hour where there was great tension in America over race, he broke through and pioneered a multicultural Church and made it normal for all colors and cultures to worship and praise God under one roof. He would even address racial issues during his preaching, calling for the preachers to stand up for the truth of God's Word that all people are equal in the sight of our Creator.

While we have come far in the breakdown of racial barriers, one of A. A. Allen's prayers in my dream was that we would become even more united in the Church that God would indeed break down every wall of segregation in our hearts. While I know in part he was addressing the issue of race, I believe he meant more than just the color of our skin.

I believe he was praying for unity across denominational lines as well, that the Church would be united as a whole, with one sole purpose, and that Jesus Christ would be glorified in the earth.

I believe God is emphasizing this point of unity right now to take us beyond where we have been. In the coming days look for more churches to be crossing denominational lines and cross-pollinating as God shatters the walls of separation that have held us in for too long, keeping us ineffective for His Kingdom.

Pointing To the Future

In closing, **I believe this dream communicates to us God's intentions to bless us in the near future with a fresh move of God.** Heaven has a divine plan and purpose for this country. Many have been prophesying and declaring a coming Third Great Awakening here in the United States. My prayer is that this would be more confirmation to those who have been praying for this great nation and that what we have been proclaiming will come to pass.

Let us have faith that our prophetic declarations and dreams are becoming reality in this season, in Jesus' name.

Charles Shamp
Destiny Encounters
Email: info@destinyencounters.com
Website: destinyencounters.com

Charles and Brynn Shamp are the founders of Destiny Encounters. They have a true passion for reformation, revival, and the glory of God. They are fulfilling a mandate from God to preach the Gospel with miracles, signs and wonders in the nations of the earth. At the age of 18, Charles was saved from a lifestyle of drugs and alcohol after he had a life-changing experience in the glory of God. When he was in a church service he received a prophetic word which caused him to answer the call the Lord had placed on his life. That day God spoke to him about His divine purpose. Charged with a heart of the Father for the poorest of the poor, Charles and Brynn are releasing God's love to the world, seeing the captives delivered, the sick healed, and lives changed. Charles and Brynn believe that through outreach, missions, and crusade evangelism one life changed can impact a nation and transform a generation.
http://www.elijahlist.com/words/display_word.html?ID=12351

A Note to My Catholic Brethren

We need to join a Bible Study in our parishes or start one if there is none that meets at a convenient time for you. Get your family to study the Mass readings, it is a great start. The readings are wonderful, they tie the Old Testament with the Psalms and the New Testament [something prophesied in the Old Testament, in the Psalms you see it as a prayer or praise and in the New Testament it is fulfilled]. In addition, we need to study the Bible by books, subjects, and Bible characters to get an excellent overview of the Bible to see how awesome and wholesome the Bible is. There are resources - check with the Council of Catholic Bishops in your country, monasteries, convents, EWTN, and Catholic bookstores etc.

As we read and study the Bible in a structured in-depth manner we become as conversant with the Bible as our non-Catholic brethren. They hold Bible Study mid-week and on Sundays [Sunday school] before Church service. Consistent Bible study give insights about the Bible and spiritual things about life challenges and how to triumph over them.

To substantiate the dire need to study the Bible: Jesus Christ said in John 6:63, "It is the Spirit that gives life, while the flesh is of no avail. The words I have spoken to you are spirit and life." Thus, the Bible has the spirit of Christ and the life of Christ [It is sustaining the non-Catholics; I am not discounting the Eucharist not sustaining Catholics.] Jesus Christ came to fulfill the law in the Old Testament. He quoted it to defeat the devil in Matthew 4, and in other places in the New Testament. [Could you imagine the world where Catholics are steeped in the Word of God and non-Catholics Christians embrace the Eucharist as the Real Presence of Jesus and having the Blessed Virgin Mary as a help in intercessory prayer? Both acknowledging, learning and working with one another?

The Blessed Virgin Mary quoted part of Hanna's song when she gave birth to Samuel [1 Samuel 2:1-10] and part of Psalm 98 in the Magnificat.

Numerous people in the Bible quoted the Scriptures. Two in the post Biblical times who read the Scriptures and were influenced by them, who subsequently influenced society greatly were St. Jerome and Professor Albert Einstein.

St. Jerome who compiled the Bible said, "Ignorance of Scripture is ignorance of Christ." Simple and straight to the point.

Professor Albert Einstein, made many discoveries which shaped our world and the knowledge of the universe as we know it today, lead TIME magazine in 1999 to name him, "Person of the Century." In an interview he said, "As a child I received instruction in the Bible as well as the Talmud. I am a Jew, but the shining image of the Nazarene has had an overwhelming influence on me!" Asked if he accepted the historical existence of Christ, he answered: "Without a doubt no one can read the gospels without feeling the real presence of Jesus. The heartbeat of His Personality is heard in every word!" *Shalom and Israel: a message of peace in Israel's postage stamps.* © Nathanael literature distributors and Chapter Two Books, Fountain House, 3 Conduit Mews, London, S.E. 18 7AP United Kingdom. Used with Permission.

St. Paul wrote in 1 Corinthians 10:11 that the Scripture was written to show us the examples of the past, so we do not fall into the same mistakes those people made. "Now all these things happened unto them as examples, and are written for admonition, upon whom the ends of the world are come."

Finally, in some Catholic circles the Bible is not totally embraced as the Word of God. It is seen as God's words with Jewish fables. I have witnessed it in conversations. I came across it in a written form I quote, "*The New St. Joseph Sunday Missal* Volume 1, the commentary before the Year B the First Reading Sunday in Ordinary Time, Job 7:1-4, 6-7: in the framework of a folktale, Hebrew sage tries to approach the misery of suffering . If possible take time to read the prologue: Job 1:1-22. 2:1-13 and the epilogue Job 42:7-17, which constitutes the original folktale. Between those sections the author composed the poetical dialogues on the problem of suffering, but no clear solution is offered."

To refute this fallacy of Job being a Jewish folktale: See the reference of Job's character God made to Prophet Ezekiel in Ezekiel 14:12-14, "Thus the word of the LORD came to me: 'Son of man, when a land sins against Me by breaking faith, I stretch out My hand against it and break the staff of bread, I let famine loose upon it and cut off from it both man and beast; and even if these three men were in it, Noah, Daniel and Job, they could save only themselves by their virtue, says the Lord God."' Furthermore, in James 5:11, "Indeed we call blessed those who have persevered. You have heard of the perseverance of Job, and you have seen the purpose of the Lord, because "the Lord is compassionate and merciful." Above quotes ascertained the validity of the story of Job in the Bible as true and not folktale.

St. Paul wrote in 1Timothy 3:16, "All Scripture is inspired by God and useful for teaching, for refutation, for correction, and for training in righteousness; so that the one who belongs to God may be complete, equipped for every good work.

St. Peter wrote in 2 Peter 1:20-21, "Know first of all, that there is no prophecy of Scripture that is a matter of personal interpretation, for no prophecy ever came through human will; but rather human beings moved by the Holy Spirit spoke under the influence of God." Consequently, there is no room for it to be a Jewish folktale.

Let us encourage one another and embrace Bible study with a full heart and guidance from the Holy Spirit. It is said in Deuteronomy 6:5-9, "Therefore, you shall love the LORD, your God with all your heart, and with all your soul, and with all your strength. Take to heart these words which I enjoin you today. Drill them into your children. Speak to them at home and abroad, whether you are busy or at rest. Bind them at your wrist as a sign and let them be as a pendant on your forehead. Write them on the doorposts of your houses and your gates."

Franklin Covey said, "If we do not teach our children society will. And they and we will live with the results."